THE CROSS AND THE SHAME

Timo Keskitalo

ISBN 978-3-95776-200-9

VTR Publications, Gogolstr. 33, 90475 Nürnberg, Germany,
info@vtr-online.com, http://www.vtr-online.com.

Photo credits (Cover): Photo by andri onet on Unsplash

Translated from Finnish (Risti ja Häpeä, ISBN 978-951-585-335-6)
by Maritta Taylor and John Chance

CONTENTS

FOREWORD

We are about to set off on a journey that will take us far. We will travel into another culture, and into its way of seeing the world and its approach to belief in God. However, even a long journey usually starts from somewhere nearby. Therefore, I am going to start from my neighbourhood.

I remember once standing among the street crowds in Stockholm observing some Swedish people. I was wondering whether Swedes look different from Finns. As I looked at the crowds, I realised that they definitely looked Swedish. People's facial features revealed to me that I was in Sweden. But when I observed individual people more closely, each and every one of them could also easily have been Finnish. Swedes do not differ from Finns that much. When it came to the whole crowd however, there was no doubt in my mind that taken as a group it was Swedish. I stopped to ponder why was it, when observing individuals or crowds, one could reach a different conclusion?

When we meet a person from a different culture, we always meet an individual, who never completely fits into any particular definition. Descriptions of different cultures and their emphases may be dangerous, and an individual may even feel them to be offensive. On the other hand, generalisations of cultures may be very useful, and helpful in understanding the wider picture. If we don't understand the behavioural patterns of an individual from another culture, we will often tend to treat people disapprovingly. A negative attitude can be seen in our faces and words. At that point we are not reflecting Christian love towards our neighbours and maybe unable to share the Gospel in an easily receptive way. In this book, we will explore the way of thinking in Muslim cultures. Without trying to confine anyone to the limits of our definition, our aim is to give the reader useful tools for interaction with Muslims.

The main proposition of this book is that, unlike us in the Western culture, Muslims understand themselves to be part of a community, where every decision affects the whole society – contrary to what we are used to in the West. Consequently, one doesn't do anything just as oneself, rather it is the society, or at least the interest of the society, which decides about your life. A person's status and that of his/her family in a wider society is defined primarily through shame and honour. Therefore, the Gospel must be told to a Muslim through this most pivotal factor which defines the identity of a Muslim.

I hope that this book will help the reader to understand more of the communal culture of shame. When we understand another kind of culture, we will start to see in it both acceptable and unacceptable features. When we start to view the world, even just a little, from within another culture, we will also learn to examine the Gospel from the point of view of that other world view. Only then can we share the Gospel in a comprehensible and tangible way.

As Paul said to the Corinthians:

To the Jews I became like a Jew, to win the Jews; to those under the law I became like one under the law (though I myself am not under the law), so as to win those under the law; to those not having the law, became like one not having the law (though I am free from God's law but am under Christ's law, so as to win those not having the law. To the weak I became weak, to win the weak; I have become all things to all men so that by all possible means I might save some. I do this all for the sake of the Gospel that I may share in its blessings. (1 Cor 9:20–23).

As a joyous by-product, we ourselves will be able to understand the Gospel better. In the Bible, we find a new gold mine and may enjoy unbelievable treasures that we did not even know were there.

With this foreword, I wish the joy of discovery to the reader.

Autumn 2017
Timo Keskitalo

THE MESSAGE OF THE CROSS WITHIN THE CULTURE OF SHAME

Jesus, the respected Messiah

When we start talking to a Muslim, s/he will want to know how we should be addressed. A part of respectful social intercourse is the use of various titles and ranks. When you speak with a Muslim, s/he might define you as being a teacher, father, sister or somebody's wife. Only using your first name might be so difficult, that the Muslim cannot speak with you at all, unless a suitable title can be found. This is part of respectful social intercourse. You will be respected only after you have been defined through the focus of a particular community.

Christians in the West have started to regard Jesus as 'a good guy'. Mostly we address Jesus with just this one word, 'Jesus'. Muslims consider this disparaging. To a Muslim He is 'Jesus the Messiah' or 'Messiah, the Son of Mary'. Hence, Jesus too, must have a respectful title. This is not a bad thing at all. It would be good for us, too, to learn to say, for example, The Lord Jesus Christ.

Muslims generally don't know what the word Messiah means. Islam has picked up this word from Christianity without really explaining what it means. This could actually very well be the first fruitful topic of a conversation with a Muslim. In this way, we can enrich a Muslim's understanding of the term that Islam uses.

When we examine the word Messiah, we will notice that Muslims use it in the same way as a title, for example, Dr, Mr or Mrs. This is not completely wrong, as the word Messiah defines the status of Jesus. Literally however, it means anointed – a person, whose head has been anointed with fragrant olive oil.

The purpose of the anointing was to install a person into an important office, such as a king or High Priest. These positions were associated with God's promise and the expectations of the people. The people of Israel were waiting for the priest and the king promised by God, who would be holy and good. Both the priest and the king were to be mediators between God and the people. The priest was the representative of the people toward God. The priest's duty was to make sacrifices to God for the sins of the people and ask for God's forgiveness. The King's duty was to dispense justice to the people, and to lead them. The King was God's representative toward the people, representing God's truth and power.

Over the course of generations, priests and kings came and went, but none of them measured up to their task. The flow of the promises passed on by the prophets, didn't however, dry up, rather it increased the expectation even more. God would send the Messiah, who would not be a disappointment. After waiting hundreds of years, Jesus was proclaimed to be the promised Messiah, of whom all the prophets had written.

The name Messiah, in conjunction with Jesus, means that He is the fulfilment of all the expectations, and therefore that after him no-one else will be needed. Western Christianity has lost the sense of fear and holiness of God. When a Muslim realises the significance of the name Jesus the Messiah that he is using, has, it will raise a question in the heart of why the religion of Islam was then needed after the fulfilment. With this question comes the beginning of a new understanding. Therefore, it is also good for us to use the respectful expression Jesus the Messiah, or Jesus Christ. The word 'Christ' is the Greek translation from the Hebrew word 'Messiah'.

The only Gospel

The Apostle Paul taught and preached that the Gospel is one (1 Cor 4:11). The Gospel is Jesus Christ, His life, death and resurrection; everything that the Lord Jesus did and said. Therefore, in the Bible we do not have four contradicting and competing Gospels, as Muslims generally think, but four accounts of one Gospel. The Gospel is the good news about the Messiah sent by God, and who was promised and long-awaited. Through this one Messiah, God has prepared release for sinful humankind from the curse. Therefore, the Gospel can only be one.

The Gospel is even so unique that Paul, in his letter to the Galatians, declared anyone cursed, if they preached any other Gospel, even if he were "an angel from heaven" (Gal 1:8). It is interesting that Paul, in his warning, mentioned an angel proclaiming a different Gospel, as Islam receives its justification and authority from the belief that Mohammed received the Quran through an angel. Paul does not regard even an angel's mediation as any kind of proof of the truth. The proof of the truth is Jesus, who Himself is the Gospel.

On the other hand, we hear Paul speak about "my Gospel" (Rom 2:16), as if there were several Gospels. This expression, however, refers to the one and only Gospel, which Paul also preaches. Paul did, indeed, have his own personal way of expressing the universal truth of God. In the same way, we notice, how the four Gospels differ from Paul's letters. Paul's letters constitute systematic teaching on the themes of faith, the Gospels, on other hand, are stories told about the life of Jesus.

The Gospel books also differ from each other in their styles. It has been suggested that the Gospel according to Matthew has been written for a Jewish readership as it starts with the family line from Abraham and then follows on down the royal line. The Gospel according Mark gives the appearance of a book which has been written by means of dictation from the impulsive Peter, and is assumed to have been written for a Roman audience. The Gospel according to Luke is a document which was perhaps written as a court record for Paul's trial to Rome. The Gospel according to John examines matters in a later period and also harks back to the sermons of Jesus. The Gospel has, therefore, been recorded in many forms.

Paul explains this principle in his letter to the Corinthians. He explains that he is trying to shape the Gospel according to the receiver, and to be like a Jew to the Jews and a Greek to the Greek. For the sake of the Gospel he is everything to everyone, to save as many as possible (1 Cor 9:19–22).

The Gospel, therefore, must be clothed in accordance with the costume of the recipient, for it to be more comprehensible, and to ease its acceptance. The basis of this principle is the incarnation of Jesus Christ. God became a man and brought salvation to us. Jesus says in the Great Commission in the Gospel of John that he will send us, just as the Father sent Him. Therefore, we are also sent to learn to live in the culture and worldview of the recipients of the Gospel, in order for the Gospel to become part of the recipient's life.

Hymns set in a minor key agree with the Finnish mind set. We do not identify with successful heroes as the Americans do. Even in our jokes we laugh at mad Finns rather than at Swedes or Russians. Presenting the Gospel in our particular way suits us. When Albin Savola, one of the first Finnish missionaries, was starting his work in Ovamboland in Africa, he wrote that "he had to learn the language, customs and beliefs in order to find in the hearts of the heathen a connecting point which God's word would touch".[1]

In this way, we can also look for sensitive features within Muslim cultures, through which the Gospel will affect and become understandable.

To clothe the Gospel in the costumes of other cultures, we will first have to understand these cultures. Cultures are an unending source of different kinds of features, values and behaviour patterns. To begin to understand the culture, matters need first to be made simple and plain. Paul, in his letter to the Corinthians, makes the ultimate simplification when he classifies the world's cultures into two groups: the Jews and the Greeks. The Greeks

---

1 Albin Savola, Martti Rautanen, Helsinki, SLS, 1927, p. 20.

search for wisdom and the Jews for a sign. This classification continues to be surprisingly practical. Western culture aims to be objective, intellectual and efficient, just as the Greeks of that time. Asian and African cultures emphasise the supernatural, honour and power, as did the Jews of that time. Paul states that the message of the cross of Jesus conflicts with both of these basic cultures. For some the cross is foolishness and absurd, for others a scandal and a shame. (1 Cor 1:23)

For a Western rational person, the message of the cross of Jesus sounds barbaric and irrelevant. Within Islam, the message of the cross is simply too shameful and insulting. However, because the cross is the wisdom and power of God, we cannot but proclaim this cross. Therefore, Paul encourages us to proclaim to a Muslim that which most acutely offends him as a Muslim. We do not bargain about the cross, even though the Gospel otherwise may be 'packaged' for a particular culture. In fact, Paul seems to say that Christ crucified must be proclaimed in a way that is most offending. We are allowed to be offended by the cross.

Three aspects

We are reading this book within a Western culture, but that is by no means the world's only principal culture. Eugene Nida mentioned in his book Customs and Cultures that the world's cultures can be understood through three main cultural features. These three main features are fear, guilt and shame. Naturally, these three main elements are present in all cultures, but their importance varies. A culture where fear is the primary principle, shows up very differently compared to a culture in which guilt guides values. "We have to reckon with these different types of reactions to transgression of religiously sanctioned codes: fear, shame, and guilt."[2]

These three guiding principles of cultures will take shape even more clearly, if we try to define the opposite pairs for them. Fear, guilt and shame are all matters which we aim to either avoid, or whose influence we try to remove. They are, therefore negative, and values that we wish to push away. Their opposites are, therefore desirable and valuable. Fear can be contrasted with power and strength. Guilt is contrasted with freedom or justice. Shame is quite obviously clearly contrasted with honour.

The environment of Islam is without a doubt a culture of shame and honour. For us Western Christians, whether from a Protestant or Catholic tradition, the most crucial question is guilt and being set free from it. In the Protestant

---

2 Eugene Nida, Customs and Cultures, 1954, p. 150.

tradition, the matter culminates in the justification of a sinner. If we try to offer this question, crystallised within our own culture, to a Muslim who comes from the culture of shame and honour, the message we offer is naturally alien and difficult to accept.

We are heirs of Western Christianity. Martin Luther, the Reformer, drew from the writings of Augustine – he was, after all, an Augustinian monk within the Roman Catholic Church. Augustine, on the other hand, found the grace of God from the writings of Paul. Augustine examines the spiritual mind-set of an individual before God. Thus, this truth became the actual treasure of the Reformation: a sinner is justified only by the grace of God, only through faith in Jesus Christ. Luther, haunted by guilt, aiming to please God, finally found the solution in Paul's letter to the Romans: This truth became the real treasure of the Reformation: a sinner is justified only by the grace of God, only through faith in Jesus Christ. God bestows his own righteousness to those who believe in Jesus. A sinner is acceptable to God because of the atoning sacrifice of Jesus.

When encountering a Muslim, or any other Asian neighbour, this treasure of the Reformation may not always be the best way of approach.

They will find it difficult to empathise with the format of the question setting from the reformation. The question about sin and being good enough for God is not such a burning issue for them as it was to Luther. Therefore, we will first have to define the question of the Muslim culture in order to be able to give an answer from the Gospel to their question.

Can we then find such a central question setting in the Muslim worldview to which the Gospel would be the answer? Or is the Western culture so unique with its issue of guilt that other cultures just have to learn to ask our questions, in order to receive the gospel as their correct answer? I dare to claim that Muslims have as invaluable a question rising within their own culture to which the Gospel will give an equally obvious answer.

If we try to set these three cultural spheres on the world map, we will notice that the culture of fear is manifested most clearly in the African and Latin American regions. On these two continents, leadership is based on power, which is maintained through fear. Strength is idealised. Within the culture of fear, the Gospel manifests as Christ the victor. The Lord Jesus has conquered death and the powers of darkness. The Gospel preacher must show that in the name of Jesus Christ there is power that overcomes the power of those manipulating the spirits. In these cultures, prayers of Christians are loud and even aggressive. In these areas Christianity often manifests as Charismatic and centred on the leader.

The great spiritual leaders also have to display their power and success. The core of the Gospel for them is that Christ the King sits on his throne.[3]

The Culture of guilt is to be found in Europe, North America, Australia and New Zealand. The Protestant Reformation typifies this culture, as pointed out earlier. The theme of guilt and justice is repeated in literature and films. Each major story in our culture is a fight to prove innocence, forgiveness and justice such as, for example the book Les Miserables by Victor Hugo. As we follow American TV series we can become easily convinced that Americans spend a quarter of their lifetime in a courtroom. This is of course not true. Our culture, however, emphasises guilt so strongly that life is examined, as it were, from the point of view of a courtroom.

It is natural that the Gospel, within our culture, is conveyed to people through the depiction of God as a judge, in front of whom we sinners stand accused based upon the law. Jesus Christ, as a substitutional sacrifice, however sets us free on the basis of undeserved justification by grace. In our case the Gospel declares us innocent and justified in God's eyes.

The largest area by land surface and population in the world belongs to the sphere of the culture of shame. The culture of shame covers the whole Islamic world from Morocco to Indonesia.

In addition, the Japanese culture has its own type of culture of shame, where a person's greatest loss is to lose face in front of others. Therefore, a Japanese businessman may commit suicide if his business fails. In the Far East culture people find it difficult to say 'no', because declining a task or refusing an agreement would be too shameful. In the Chinese culture, it is not allowed to report a student for cheating, because getting caught might destroy his whole life. Death sentences in these cultures are regarded as merciful.

Remarks parents use to discipline children reflect, in an amusing way, these three main cultures. We might say: "It's wrong, does not your conscience

---

3 This assessment of the range of influence of the culture of fear is based on my own estimation with 15 years of experience as a pastor in an international church. Global Mapping International has prepared an Internet-based interview study, according to which the culture of shame is the greatest dominant culture covering, apart from Asia, also most of Latin America and Africa. The culture of fear would then, according to that study, dominate in only small pockets in Africa. I presume that at the time of preparing the questions of the study, the most elusive features of the culture of fear have not been captured and therefore those answering the questionnaire have not recognised themselves in it. Data from TheCultureTest.com (Feb 2017). Map by Global Mapping International – www.gmi.org.

tell you so!" To this rebuke from within a culture of blame, a child coming from a culture of shame might reply: "But I did it for our best interests." A mother from the culture of fear warns her disobedient child: "An evil witch will come and take you away, how dare you!" A rebuke from a mother from the culture of shame could say: "What will people say, shame on you!" A child from a culture of blame might answer to this rebuke: "But I didn't do anything wrong!"

In a Muslim village, there is said to be a set amount of honour, which is shared between the village families. Honour and shame are present within families. A family's honour lessens or is lost completely through shameful deeds, whereas by means of honourable deeds more honour is earned and transferred to one's family and relatives. Honour and shame can even be inherited from generation to generation. Honour can also be increased by performing a pilgrimage, learning the Quran by heart, sacrificing oneself in a war for Islam or by showing hospitality. When a man has taken part in the pilgrimage to Mecca, the title Hajj is added to his name and immediately he is credited more worth the community. At the same time his family and relatives too will receive more appreciation. His seat at communal meetings is raised a few notches higher. However, we will notice that at the same time the seat of everybody else will go down by one notch.

When a son learns the Quran by heart, people remember to mention this in all communal meetings. The family benefits from the son's wisdom. In the same way, martyrdom in religious families is not treated as a loss, but rather as an investment. A father or mother who has lost a son might say that he or she will gladly sacrifice even more sons to die for Islam. We will look at these phenomena as a means of talking about the Gospel later in this book. The purpose of this book is to consider how the Gospel is presented to a person from a culture of shame, and not to get stuck with pondering what, in these kinds of cultural features, may be right or wrong.

Shame is in the Bible

Shame is a central theme in the Bible. Geographically the Bible was written at the junction of three cultures, i.e. European, Asian and African. The main emphasis of the Bible lies, however, on the Asian side, so shame must, fundamentally, be centrally present in the texts of the Bible. On the other hand, we naturally tend to focus our reading on what is familiar and appealing in any text. For this reason, we Western Christians have not generally noticed the theme of shame as often as it appears in the Bible – although recently many books have been written on this theme. We read the Bible through the glasses of our own culture, and our glasses have a particular tint; let's say that the glasses of the culture of guilt have a blue tint to them.

In order to read the Bible so that we can see the tints of the culture of fear, our glasses should have a red tint. In order to read the Bible with a Muslim we need glasses that have a yellow tint. Blue, red and yellow are three primary colours – in the same way as guilt, fear and shame represent the main cultural groups. To see the whole spectrum of colours, we need these three primary colours. Now we just must try on yellow glasses and see if we can really detect the culture of shame in the Bible in a central place.

The Bible, indeed, is not a product of the Western culture, and therefore it should be high time to examine the Bible through the culture of shame. A large part of Western culture derives from the Bible; however, it would be against historical facts to claim that the Bible is Western. The actual miracle of the Bible is in the fact, that it is not just a product of the culture of shame, but of all the three cultures are present in the Bible.

Let us consider the tension between communal and individualistic cultures. These two cultural emphases contrast so sharply that in Islamic cultures one cannot readily concur with the United Nations' declaration of human rights, because human rights are essentially the rights of an individual. In the Islamic culture the community is always more important than an individual. In the declaration of the human rights, the rights of an individual are declared over the rights of a community. Therefore, Muslims have created their own Cairo Declaration[4], in which communal rights are emphasised over those of an individual. Within the Bible, according to cultural context, the rights of community should be found in a dominant position. And indeed, we do come across communal rights in the Bible presented to the extent of offending the Western fanatical individuality.

The Bible talks about guilt as being both communal and hereditary. The Bible also talks about salvation, which comes to a family unit. Even, at the end of the Gospel of Matthew, nations, not individuals, are the object of the Great Commission (Matt 28:19). Jesus is the King, and his kingdom, indeed, is not a private matter. Burying the king's talents in the ground is a punishable deed (Matt 25:14–30). We must publicly do business in the service of our king in the midst of this world. Due to our own cultural environment, we are blind to the communality in these Bible passages, or alternatively we will simply explain away the emphases of these passages. In fact, it is entirely feasible to see communal thinking in the Bible.

The real surprise, however, is the strong emphasis of individuality in the Bible. The tendency of Old Testament stories to introduce initially completely

---

[4] Cairo Declaration on Human Rights in Islam, Aug. 5, 1990, U.N. GAOR, World Conf. on Hum. Rts., 4th Sess., Agenda Item 5, U.N. Doc. A/CONF.157/PC/62/Add.18 (1993).

insignificant individuals, is revolutionary. The stories, for example regarding Rahab and Ruth are truly astonishing. The way Jesus met individuals, who had no value in the community, is radical. Consequently, we can see that the declaration of the human rights would not have been able to come into being without the value of an individual as presented in the Bible. Western culture has taken this importance of individuality to unhealthy extremes. We have forgotten the value of society. The Bible ought to be the remedy to find the balance.

If the Bible, indeed, is God's revelation to all humankind, we should then be able to find all three cultures in the Bible; fear, guilt and shame beautifully balanced. If we wish to read the whole message of the Bible, it is high time for us to start reading the Bible also being aware of the concept of shame. In this way, our view will become enriched. In the same way that photographs must have the primary colours blue, red and yellow in balance in order to display a balanced colouring and everything that is essential, we too must also make use of the whole cultural palette.

Our perception will become sharper, if we can see the message of the Bible from more than one point of view. For example, looking through just one eye we might see sharply, but as we look through two eyes the intersectional point will give us a range of vision informing us of the distance and the speed of an approaching object. Looking through both eyes provides depth and perspective to everything.

We can also think that these three cultures as being three focal points. If we view the message of the Bible from only one point, our image will be two-dimensional. If we use two viewing points, we can add the range of depth into the picture, and the Bible will become three-dimensional. A third view point can be compared to being able to walk around the object of our interest and observing it from all sides.

Are we willing to read the Bible being aware of the concept of shame? Shame has sometimes been stigmatised even as a destructive feeling. Shame has usually been viewed mainly through psychology, and it has been discovered that shame focuses on an individual in a way which is extremely damaging. Shaking off shame, and encouraging one to rise above it, have been offered as answers to this. In fact, pushing the shame aside will result in us being even more captives of shame. In Western culture advocates of the majority opinion, pressurise minorities through public means of shame. Repressing shame is also common also within our Christian dialogue and teaching.

Shame is, however, one of the feelings created by God. Shame protects us. It is right to feel ashamed. Shame is a positive issue in the same way as guilt. If a person cannot feel guilt, he is sick and dangerous. In the same way, a person without shame is broken. In the same way, when we might feel false guilt in front of people, we might also feel false and damaging shame. Before God both guilt and shame will become "calibrated" into correct proportions. Our natural feelings of shame draw on others' opinions about us. But, what does God say? The crucial point in the end is whether we end up ashamed before God. If Jesus puts in a defensive word before God for us, our shame has become covered. We have been made righteous.

When we encounter a Muslim, this challenges us to rethink. Could it be that shame, in the same way as guilt, is a functional concept? What, if we don't even have to suppress shame, but instead face it headlong? What, if the full understanding of the Gospel demands us to face shame directly, without yielding? If the biblical answer to guilt is forgiveness, what is the biblical answer to shame? If we reject shame, we will leave those within the culture of shame without an answer – therefore without the Gospel.

The first miracle of Jesus

Let us dive inside the Bible text from the beginning of The New Testament. The Gospels tell us briefly about the birth of Jesus, pass by his childhood and youth, and the actual narration starts from the public ministry of Jesus Christ. The first miracle of our Lord Jesus Christ took place at the wedding in Cana. To start with, we notice that the Bible, indeed, states that this was his first miracle. Islam, on the other hand, tells about three miracles, which happened before this.

When baby Jesus was born, he didn't cry, unlike all other new-born babies. This story found in Hadith shows the sinlessness and purity of Jesus according to the Islamic interpretation. Babies cry out at birth because Satan pokes the child.[5]

Satan, however, did not have the authority to touch Jesus. The conclusion is, therefore quite correct; Jesus, indeed, was the only sinless person at birth. The basis for this conclusion is not, however correct. We know from the Bible that Jesus cried at the grave of Lazarus. Therefore, it is natural to assume that Jesus also cried, when He was born, although despite crying, He was sinless and holy.

The second miracle is related to Mary's shame about the fact that she was not married, when she became pregnant. The Quran tells, that when Mary had given birth, people gathered to accuse her of dishonour and demanded Mary's father to bear the responsibility for what had happened. Then

---

[5] Shahih Al-Bukhari Hadith, Hadith 4.506.

suddenly the new-born Jesus speaks from his cradle and defends his mother's honour (Quran 19:30).[6] It is interesting to note how seriously Mary's shame is regarded in Middle Eastern culture. From this we learn something relevant about the burden that Mary had to carry, although the Bible does not mention the miracle that was claimed.

The third miracle according to Islam happened in Jesus' childhood. The account which has come from an unreliable gospel, The Infancy Gospel of Thomas, describes how the child Jesus picked up clay and formed a bird from it. When the birds of other children were just clay, the bird of Jesus took wing (Quran 5:110). This portrayal of Jesus as the creator of life is excellent, but the story in itself is not true. In fact, the description of the childhood of Jesus in The Infancy Gospel of Thomas is abhorrent. Jesus, according to that story, is a brat with supernatural abilities, and a danger to other children.[7]

When the Bible asserts, that the Lord Jesus performed his first miracle, it means that those previously-claimed miracles are just well-meaning fairy tales. Now that we have mirrored the incident of the Wedding at Cana into Islamic tradition, let us look at the story and the wedding.

> *On the third day a wedding took place at Cana in Galilee. Jesus' mother was there, and Jesus and his disciples had also been invited to the wedding. When the wine was gone, Jesus' mother said to him, "They have no more wine." Dear woman, why do you involve me?" Jesus replied. "My time has not yet come." His mother said to the servants, "Do whatever he tells you." Nearby stood six stone water jars, the kind used by the Jews for ceremonial washing, each holding from twenty to thirty gallons. Jesus said to the servants, "Fill the jars with water"; so, they filled them to the brim. Then he told them, "Now draw some out and take it to the master of the banquet."*

---

[6] In this book there are many references to the Quran, The Holy Book of Islam, and to Hadith, the collection of Islamic tradition. With these references I do not want to claim that these writings should have any authority concerning Christian about faith and truth. Neither do I quote these texts to show Islamic writings to be erroneous or untrustworthy. Nor do I try to interpret Islamic writings – that right belongs to the Islamic community. I have referred to the Quran and Hadith, for the reader to have some background knowledge of what Muslims believe.

[7] The earliest versions of the Infancy Gospel of Thomas were written around 250 AD, although the text has continued to be modified after that. It is therefore, clear that this book is of a later origin than the New Testament books. This book has never been regarded as belonging to the holy writings. The earliest version was probably written in Syria. Ronald F. Hock, The Infancy Gospels of James and Thomas: With Introduction, Notes, and Original Text Featuring the New Scholars Version Translation (Polebridge Press 1996).

> *They did so, and the master of the banquet tasted the water that had been turned into wine. He did not realise where it had come from, though the servants who had drawn the water knew. Then he called the bridegroom aside and said, "Everyone brings out the choice wine first and then the cheaper wine after the quests have had too much to drink; but you have saved the best till now." This, the first of his miraculous signs, Jesus performed in Cana of Galilee. He thus revealed his glory and his disciples put their faith in him* (John 2:1–11).

As Bible readers, we might be surprised by this incident. Why was it necessary to record it in the Bible? The Gospel of John does mention that there would have been an enormous amount of material and only a small part has been chosen to the Gospel: Jesus did many other things as well. If every one of them were written down, I suppose that even the whole world would not have room for the books that would be written (John 21:25). In this story, however, there are no healings mentioned, no-one is forgiven for their sins or receives salvation, nor does Jesus particularly teach anything. Why is this story in the Bible at all? Has the writer of the Gospel made an error in his assessment, when he chose this story to be included in his book?

The Lord Jesus has been invited to the wedding along with his disciples. It is not particularly clear to us, whether it is a family wedding, or whether the whole neighbourhood is involved in the wedding. Mary, the mother of Jesus, seems to have a role in the kitchen, because she notices the problem with the serving. In the Middle East culture hospitality is an extremely important matter. A wedding reveals the essence of hospitality.

In Jewish weddings serving wine plays an essential part. To run out of wine would have been the ultimate shame. If that had happened, this wedding would have been remembered for decades. There would have been stories told about the wedding where the wine ran out, people would have been shocked, and would have jeered laughingly at the story. This story of shame would have had a long history. Therefore, Mary, the mother of Jesus becomes worried about the situation and frantically wants to find a solution.

The Lord Jesus replies to his mother harshly and calls her 'woman'. His use of this expression cannot be just pushed away. Jesus clearly speaks against the grain. There must be a reason for this fact. Jesus states that his hour has not yet come. When did his hour come then? When our Lord Jesus is arrested, He says his hour has come (Mark 14:41). However, this hour is the hour of darkness.

When Jesus institutes the Holy Communion, He talks about another hour. Jesus says he will come back to enjoy the fruit of the vine only when He returns to his Kingdom (Matt 26:29).

The fulfilment of the communion meal will take place in the heavenly wedding. In the thanksgiving prayer after the Communion we request that we might be granted to join the Great Communion in heaven. The wedding in Cana was not yet the wedding of Jesus. In the Cana wedding Jesus is not the responsible host. The wedding of Jesus will only be in heaven. The host of the wedding in Cana was the bridegroom. This is shown through the conversation where the master of banquet tastes the wine and goes to thank the bridegroom for saving the best wine for last. The bridegroom thus received the honour, or shame, resulting from the wine served. Jesus thus saved the bridegroom from shame.

We find out that the wedding in Cana is, after all, a story of salvation. Yet, this salvation does not represent a salvation story according to our culture of guilt. No-one was forgiven for their sins. Instead, here we have a clear account of salvation according to the culture of shame. The bridegroom is so discreetly saved from shame that even the master of banquet does not notice any problem. Shame is covered – it is not revealed. The bridegroom's face is saved in front of the community. In addition, a view of heavenly glory is revealed to us; this is the final solution to the problem of shame. All honour belongs to Jesus in the heavenly feast. He will cover us with his glory in the wedding where the church is his bride. He will wash and cleanse us so, that there will be no shameful stain or wrinkle (Eph 5:27).

If this first miracle of Jesus speaks particularly to those within the culture of shame, and we have not noticed this, should we not really stop and ponder why? Is there such a layer, vein or a big story in the Bible which we, constrained by our own culture, have not previously been able to detect? If this is so, it is high time for us to start reading the Bible with a new and wider understanding.

Does this then, imply that the account of the wedding in Cana would be an excellent gospel story for the people of the culture of shame? When discussing with a Muslim, perhaps we would not first choose this account. The fact, that Jesus prepares hundreds of litres of wine, might not seem very wise within the Muslim culture, where wine is an absolutely prohibited, even demonic, substance.

Considering the matter more carefully, it may not, after all, be ruled out even within the Muslim culture. Wine, surprisingly, has a very positive meaning within Islam. In paradise, it is told that wine will pour forth from fountains. The fortunate Muslim, who will attain eternal life in paradise, may enjoy wine without any headache after drinking. Wine then, in Islam, reflects the bliss and happiness of eternal life. Its time, though, has not yet come. Although the account about the wedding in Cana might startle and even offend Muslims, it is still an excellent Biblical passage to be read with a Muslim. In his first miracle Jesus Christ acts to redeem shame.

The Awful Honour

We are accustomed to judge cultural behaviour which is guided by honour and shame. In the media or mission forums, the examples presented of the culture of shame are, almost without exception, negative. Veiling of women plays a major symbolic role. To us, the veil symbolises a prison. The veil limits the freedom of women. This is, of course, completely true, as some of Muslim women feel in this way. In certain Kurdish dialects, the word for wife is "a shame". This is considered a decent and protective expression. We will notice that the covering which defends morals, and seeing a woman as just filthiness, fatefully merge together.

On the other hand, the veil might be a shield, and offer freedom. Women wearing a veil is not only protection when it comes to strange men's covetous looks: the veil is also the glory of her own husband. The Bible confirms the principle that a woman is the husband's glory (1 Cor 11:7). The Bible, therefore, demands us to examine this matter in more detail. We ought to be brave and look behind this incriminating thinking and try to find positive aspects of the veil.

For many women wearing a veil symbolises high morals. It is a message to the surrounding community, that the one wearing a veil has a positive attitude to religion, marriage and family. Wife ought to have a symbol of authority on her head, says Paul (1 Cor 11:10). Authority and submission describes a community with a particular structure and hierarchy. The woman is honoured as part of the community. An unveiled woman is without honour and the protection of the community.

The culture of shame is manifested in many different contexts – for example in how girls sit when there is a grandmother present. Then, it is not fitting to cross the feet in a casual way, but nicely side by side, in order to honour the grandmother. A son rebelling against his parents might be removed from the family. To refuse an arranged marriage might end up being an act which will cause the son to lose his right to be a family member. It is a shame for a girl's family if she is raped. Instead of finding the culprit and punishing him, the family might kill their own daughter. The solution of a problem in a culture of shame is not aimed at the one who is guilty, but at the one who is carrying the shame. When the father or older brother of the family has killed the raped daughter, the shame has been eliminated and everything is fine again.

A vendetta might demand killings between two families over several generations. Honour always demands another killing of a new opponent. The killings always target an innocent individual, in order to restore honour. We will examine these phenomena through the Gospel's point of view later in this book.

We abhor all these behavioural patterns. We feel a strong need to judge and protest any form of activity relating to shame. We cannot understand the inner logic of the shame and regard these deeds as barbaric. The aim of this book is not to try to get the reader to accept these violent or degrading features of the culture of shame. The aim is, however, intended to gain understanding for some of the reasons behind this behaviour, and to be willing to examine the matters from the point of view of the culture of shame. If we are offended and not willing to examine the world through the culture of shame we, in fact, will merely understand the Bible message partly. Therefore, it is absolutely essential for us to venture into areas that are unfamiliar to us. In all forms of the culture of shame, there is hidden a seed of the Gospel.

The awful cross

St. Paul understood the offensiveness of the cross within the Jewish context. After succeeding in crucifying Jesus, the Jews, in a sense, were assured that they had acted in a correct way: If Jesus really had been the Messiah of God, they, according to themselves, could not have crucified Him. When the believers, however, continued to claim the crucified one as the Messiah, the message of the crucified Messiah was an utmost scandal to the Jews.

St. Paul is not trying to hide this offense but proclaims it without shame in full scale. Paul teaches us that this most offensive matter is, in fact, the power of God. At the same time as St. Paul in his preaching, aims to fit the Gospel message into different cultures, he also concentrates on the most offensive matter, i.e. Christ crucified. It seems as if he would enjoy causing maximum outrage. He writes in his letter to the Corinthians, that he is acting in this way both with the Jews and Greeks (1 Cor 1:23). This same pattern may then suffice when talking to Muslims.

Islam denies the death of the Messiah on the cross. This is astonishing as of all the Bible stories, the death of Jesus is the strongest historically proven fact compared to any other fact in the Bible. The death of Jesus on the cross has for example, been mentioned in the writings of the Jewish historian Josephus in the first century, in the writings of the Roman historian Tacitus at the beginning of the second century, and in the writings of the Greek satirist Lucian in the second century. Islam accepts most Biblical events, however this central issue Islam denies against all historical evidence.

A Quranic text states that it looked like the Jews crucified Jesus, although they had no right to crucify him (Quran 4:156–157). As neutral readers, we could interpret the meaning of the text to be that the crucifixion in the end was not in the hands of the Jews or any other people, but that God himself decided to sacrifice Jesus in this way as a sin offering. Our task is not, however, to interpret the Quran in our own way. Muslims have their own tradition about interpreting the Quran, and they have the right to interpret their own book as they wish. The Islamic understanding is that Jesus did not die on the cross. The Quran just states the matter briefly without any explanations. An inquisitive mind, however, wants to know what they say happened instead. The Islamic tradition consists of several traditional parallel accounts of what happened instead of Jesus dying on the cross. The most popular account claims that God made Judas look like Jesus, so that the soldiers who came to arrest Jesus, instead captured Judas and nailed him on the cross. The story then had a happy and just ending. Another account tells how Jesus came to the upper room in the middle of the disciples and asked for one volunteer. He then chose one from amongst the eager disciples, who was crucified instead of Jesus.[8]

Why then do Muslims reject the crucifixion? It has often been claimed that Islam cannot accept a killing of a prophet. This, however, cannot be the case. Islam recognises killings of other, earlier prophets. Mohamed also, in the end, was murdered according to Sira, the biography literature of the prophet of Islam. The issue then is not the murder of a prophet. The issue for Islam is in that the death on the cross is an extremely shameful death. Islam holds Jesus in high regard and honour. Muslims cannot accept that a prophet of such high distinction would have suffered such a shameful death. Muslims, therefore, reject the death on the cross for a very good reason. Could it even be that they have understood a death on the cross better than us? Ultimately, they are offended by the cross just like the Jews but draw the opposite conclusion. Whereas most of the Jewish nation decided, based on the cross, that Jesus cannot be the Messiah, Muslims believe that Jesus was the Messiah. Therefore, they decided, that He could not have died on the cross. For us the cross has become so familiar and safe, that we do not completely understand “the offence of the cross” (skandalon tou staurou), that Paul talks about in his letter (Gal 5:11). According to Paul’s example we will have to then proclaim precisely this offending message of the cross of Jesus to Muslims. The politically correct and culturally sensitive concealing of the cross is the worst that we could do. By doing this, we will deny

8 The account of the crucifixion of Judas can be found in a European mediaeval Gospel forgery called the Gospel of Barnabas, chapter 112. The finding of a volunteer can be found in an older Quranic commentary Al-Nasa’i, Al-Kubra, 6:489 by Ibn Kathir.

Muslims the good news. At the same time, it will become obscure to us as well. Observing how great an offence the cross is for a Muslim, we ourselves can better understand the meaning of the cross.

The Shame of the Cross

It is important to consider the death on the cross of our Lord Jesus through the eyes of a Muslim, to better understand the Bible. A Western person primarily perceives the bodily suffering of a death on a cross. We read in the Bible account details about the whipping, the crown of thorns and the nails. We concentrate on the great suffering. Concentrating on this physical suffering has been taken to the extreme in the film Passion of Christ where the sufferings on the cross have been portrayed in a most realistic way. At the same time the telling of the story remains in an odd way one-dimensional. We could say that the flaw is the script, i.e. the Gospels which describe the death on the cross in a very documentary way.

The theological implications are only shown in more detail in the New Testament letters. Based on the teaching of the letters we understand that Jesus, as a substitute sacrifice pays for our sins on the cross. We are not able to examine the actual inner feelings of Jesus through the New Testament texts. On the Cross, Jesus gives us some small clues into his inner world. When Jesus Christ cries out *"Eloi, Eloi lama sabachtani?"* He gives us a clue of what is happening to Him right there.

The innermost feelings of Jesus can be found in Psalm 22, where these words open the text. The Psalm tells us about the spiritual battles in the realms and powers of heaven and earth through animal form; the attack by oxen, dogs and lions, that Jesus went through in his heart on the cross. At the point where his breath is obstructed and in extreme pain, he does not have enough strength to hold teaching lessons. The opening words of the Psalm formed a quick message to the Jews who were familiar with the Scriptures: read there, to see how I am feeling right now.

The Gospels do tell us, however, something of the sufferings on the cross that we might not have noticed. The cross was, above all, a punishment of shame. Jesus told his disciples in advance about his upcoming suffering in this way: "He will be turned over to the Gentiles. They will mock him, insult him, spit on him, flog him and kill him. On the third day he will rise again." (Luke 18:32–33). The element of shame is uppermost in this account. Bodily suffering will comes finally as the end of shame. The crucifixion happened outside the city gate – i.e. at the crossroads of traffic, so that as many as possible would be forced to see the shameful treatment. The letter to the Hebrews stresses this element when it says: "Jesus suffered and died outside the city gate… bearing the disgrace he bore" (see Heb 13:12–13). A public place of execution has a clear aim: "Those who passed by hurled insults at him" (see Mark 15:29).

From the point of view of a communal culture of shame, the punishment of shame is a much more cruel matter compared to bodily torture. When a Pakistani friend of mine told me how his mother had taken her shoe off her foot and hit him with it I, at first, did not completely understand the shock of the matter. When looking at the matter from the point of view of pain, it did not seem such a serious punishment. When I understood that hitting with a shoe is, in their culture, the ultimate insult, it started to feel even cruel. How could a mother treat her own son in that way?

An Iranian friend of mine told me how he had witnessed several hangings in his home country. He said that people are invited to watch a public hanging. The crime victims derive satisfaction from the fact that the one who had caused their sufferings and loss is shamed in this public way. In Iran, the one sentenced to be hanged might even be stripped to emphasise shame. In a culture where covering nakedness is of utmost importance, stripping is an extremely cruel public shame. We cannot quite understand this, as in our own culture there are people, who undress publicly and quite voluntarily.

On the other hand, violent nakedness is an abhorrent matter also in our culture. I have an indelible memory from my own childhood how in some squabbles within a group of boys, a boy was publicly shamed. His trousers were pulled down and girls were invited to watch the shamed naked boy. It was worse than being beaten. As Western people, we however, live in the middle of a culture which is without honour and shame. Nevertheless, we can still make an attempt to view the suffering on the cross through the eyes of a Muslim.

We can also empathise with Mary at the cross of Jesus. A mother who naturally would want to be proud of her son, carries the shame of the son. Each stone and spit of those passing by, hurt the mother as well. The Bible does not directly say that our Lord Jesus Christ was naked, however, indirectly we are told that the soldiers cast lots for his undergarment. When his undergarment is taken, what is left is a naked Jesus. Not even our modern Jesus films have been brave enough to depict the shame of his nakedness. It is too shameful. Nevertheless, the Bible describes this to us.

Nude crucifixes are also very rare. Generally, Jesus is pictured as having a kind of a loincloth. In the Sacrada Familia Church in Barcelona, Spain there can be found above the entrance a small crucifix depicting a naked Jesus. It is doubtful there are many such similar realistic crucifixes in the world. Our sense of shame prevents any kind of realistic description. Now we are getting closer to the aversion and defiance which Muslims feel concerning the death on the cross. I argue that we will not have properly understood the cross until we come to the point that we want to reject it.

The beginning of shame

To reach the actual roots of shame, we should examine when this word appears for the first time in a Biblical text. It does not take long to search for this word. It can be found in the second and third chapters of the first book, in the story of The Fall.

> *The man and his wife were both naked, and they felt no shame.*
>
> *Now the serpent was craftier than any of the wild animals the Lord God had made. He said to the woman, "Did God really say, 'You must not eat from any tree in the garden'?" The woman said to the serpent, "We may eat fruit from the trees in the garden, but God did say, 'You must not eat fruit from the tree that is in the middle of the garden, and you must not touch it, or you will die.'"*
>
> *"You will not surely die," the serpent said to the woman. "For God knows that when you eat of it your eyes will be opened, and you will be like God, knowing good and evil." When the woman saw that the fruit of the tree was good for food and pleasing to the eye, and also desirable for gaining wisdom, she took some and ate it. She also gave some to her husband, who was with her, and he ate it. Then the eyes of both of them were opened, and they realised that they were naked; so they sewed fig leaves together and made coverings for themselves.*
>
> *Then the man and his wife heard the sound of the Lord God as he was walking in the garden in the cool of the day, and they hid from the Lord God among the trees of the garden. But the Lord God called to the man, "Where are you?" He answered, "I heard you in the garden, and I was afraid because I was naked; so I hid." And he said, "Who told you that you were naked? Have you eaten from the tree from which I commanded you not to eat?" The man said, "The woman you put here with me – she gave me some fruit from the tree, and I ate it." Then the Lord God said to the woman, "What is this you have done?" The woman said, "The serpent deceived me, and I ate." So the Lord God said to the serpent: "Because you have done this, Cursed are you above all the livestock and all the wild animals. You will crawl on your belly and you will eat dust all the days of your life. And I will put enmity between you and the woman, and between your offspring and hers; he will crush your head and you will strike his heel."*
>
> *To the woman he said, "I will great increase your pains the childbearing; with pain you will give birth to children. Your desire will be for your*

husband he will rule over you. And to Adam he said, "Because you listened to your wife and ate from the tree about which I commanded you, 'You must not eat of it,' "Cursed is the ground because of you; through painful toil you will eat of it all the days of your life. It will produce thorns and thistles for you, and you will eat the plants of the field. By the seat of your brow you will eat your food until you return to the ground, since from it you were taken; for dust you are and to dust you will return."

Adam named his wife Eve, because she would become the mother of all the living. The Lord God made garments of skin for Adam and his wife and clothed them. And the Lord God said, "The man has now become like one of us," knowing good and evil. He must not be allowed to reach out his hand and take also from the tree of life and eat, and live forever." So the Lord God banished him from the Garden of Eden to work the ground from which he had been taken. After he drove man out, he placed on the east side of the Garden of Eden cherubim and a flaming sword flashing back and forth to guard the way to the tree of life. (Genesis 2:25–3:24)

The Fall is an excellent example of a story where all the three cultural elements are present: shame, fear and guilt. Although Adam and Eve feel all three feelings, we cannot avoid the impression that shame is the uppermost. Adam and Eve make their own attempts to overcome these three feelings. They try to overcome the feeling of shame by sewing clothes of fig leaves. There are fig leaves of slightly different shapes. Fig leaves are shaped slightly like maple leaves, although much more "bony". Fig leaves are so narrow that one cannot make a skirt that will cover sufficiently. Nor are fig leaves very comfortable, as they cause rash on your skin. This attempt was destined to fail.

It is fear that drives Adam and Eve to hide. There were certainly many good hiding places in the Garden of Eden. However, trying to hide from God is a hopeless plan. God joins the hide and seek and calls: "Adam, where are you?" Of course, God knew where Adam was hiding, but the point of this questioning might rather be to help Adam himself to understand, where he is. Driven by fear, Adam was lost from God and lost from himself as well. Adam was a prisoner in the labyrinth of fear.

Guilt is a matter which God wants to reveal. God asks Adam: "What have you done?" Adam's own attempt to solve the problem of guilt is dodging and avoidance. Instead of acknowledging his own guilt, Adam tries to blame his wife. Ultimately, Adam blames God, who gave him the wife.

This formula is still quite popular. We blame others, who have led us astray, we blame the circumstances, and in a slightly deeper consideration we question why God allowed the Fall if he is all-powerful and all-knowing. Thus we surreptitiously point the accusatory finger at God. Eve, for her part, makes the snake a scapegoat; a character representing Satan. In religious circles, we gladly blame the devil for all our indiscretions. In the end, all these avoidances are quite pitiful.

God has answers to all these three problems. The answer to shame is tangible help, to cover your nakedness. The sudden awareness of Adam's and Eve's nakedness is a mystery. The text gives us to understand, that they were naked from the beginning, but the shame of the nakedness hit them with the sin. The incident might also have deeper spiritual lessons. The letter to the Romans expresses it thus: "For all have sinned and fall short of the glory of God" (Rom 3:23). Elsewhere Paul says that he is waiting for the moment when we will be clothed in glory (1 Cor 15:12–57 and Phil 3:21).

In his Second Letter to the Corinthians, Paul describes in an interesting way the covering of the face of Moses (2 Cor 3:7–11). Every time Moses visits the Tabernacle, his face becomes radiant with the glory of God. However, that radiance starts to diminish, and in shame Moses covers this diminishing – not radiance but the lack of it. His sinful nature cannot uphold God's radiance, and so he must enter the Tabernacle again and again in order to receive more of it. As a contrast, Paul presents the radiance that comes from the face of Christ and increases in us.

Righteousness as a gift is quite different from self made righteousness. At the fall Adam and Eve lost their original righteousness and were no longer acceptable to God. No longer were they clothed in radiance and honour. With the disappearance of radiance and honour they are naked and ashamed before God. Adam and Eve's feeling of shame is real and true. Shame drives them to look for something to cover themselves with. God prepares them splendid leather clothes to replace poor covers made of leaves. I imagine them to be like motor cyclists' leather gear. Those clothes were certainly stylish and fitted well. This practical help speaks more deeply of God's ultimate purpose: God's will from the beginning was to cover the shame of our sin.

God also responds to fear. It is said that a human reacts to fear in three possible ways: attacking, escaping or freezing. Facing temptation Adam freezes. He is present when Eve is conversing with the snake, but he cannot get a word out of his mouth. When God approaches Adam, he runs away scared. Adam could have fought Satan with the obvious words from God as Jesus did when he was tempted. Or Adam could have run away from Satan together with his wife. They could have run to God. That would have been the right kind of fear of God. Instead they ran away from God.

God's answer to Adam and Eve's fear is the promise of victory. The origin of evil, Satan, will be defeated. The woman will bear a boy child, who will crush the snake's head (Gen 3:15). On the one hand God declares defeat to Satan right from the beginning. On the other hand, God declares a promise to man as a consolation. The end game is, therefore clear. Humankind has therefore never had a justifiable need to act out of fear. The promise of the power of the victory drives fear away.

God's answer to guilt is not as evident in The Fall as his answer to fear and shame. When God prepares the leather clothes for Adam and Eve, we can assume that God used animal pelts to prepare them. With sin, death came into the world. Now God is starting to show that death is not just only a necessary evil, which follows sin. Death is also part of the solution God has prepared. Therefore, it was essential that God put the cherubs to guard the gate of the paradise and to exclude people from the reach of the tree of life, so that they would not to have to live in sin forever.

The people were confined under the control of the death, for the Messiah to be able to suffer the death of atonement for our sins at the time chosen by God. The atonement for sin demands a blood sacrifice. Therefore, we can find the same cherub figures facing the central point of the lid of the Arc of the Covenant. The cherubs want to look towards the place of the blood sacrifice. Peter explains this in his letter: "Concerning this salvation, the prophets, who spoke of the grace that was to come to you, searched intently and with the greatest care, trying to find out the time and circumstances to which the spirit of Christ in them was pointing when he predicted the sufferings of Christ and the glories that would follow. It was revealed to them that they were not serving themselves but you, when they spoke of the things that have now been told you by those who have preached the gospel to you by the Holy Spirit sent from heaven. Even angels long to look into these things" (1 Peter 1:10–12).

The first sacrifice was prepared by God himself. Immediately in a following chapter, Abel sacrifices a lamb to God without anybody in any way explaining or justifying the matter. We are thus given to understand, that God had given a model for a blood sacrifice to people when he prepared the leather costumes for Adam and Eve. God's answer for guilt has, from the beginning, been an innocent substitute victim.

From this we will have to learn to join the correct answer to the correct question:

Shame – covering
Fear – victory power
Guilt – substitute sacrifice

Shame must be covered

The covering of the shame is one of the undercurrents in the Bible. It is a storyline that runs from the first pages to the very last chapters of the Bible. In the first chapters of the Bible, there is a particular story that will easily remain completely unfathomable to people of the culture of guilt. This story is about the naked Noah. After the Flood Noah becomes inspired to experiment with grape juice and manages to produce wine. Noah ends up imbibing so much that he loses control of the situation. Noah lies uncovered in his tent and finally passes out.

His son Ham is the first one to find him. Ham goes and relates the news to his brothers Shem and Japheth. The narration is scanty, although from the dynamics of the story we can deduce that Ham's way of talking about it has been mocking and revealing. Shem and Japheth, instead react respectfully, wanting to cover their father's shame. They take a garment and walk backwards to their father who is sleeping naked, and cover him without looking at him.

From the point of view of the culture of guilt the villain of the story is of course Noah. Yet, from the point of view of the culture of shame, Shem and Japheth are heroes and Ham is a baddy. Hence, Noah after waking up curses Ham's family. For some reason, the curse is directed to Canaan. Perhaps Canaan was his father's pride and joy. Perhaps Canaan was part of revealing the news along with Ham. A curse is, however, according to communal culture, directed at the family – not just individual. The moral of the story is that God does not want to promote shameful revelations, but his heart's attitude is to cover shame. He covers so discreetly, that we sinners do not even realise our shame. We have already been covered, when we wake up, like Noah.[9]

In the New Testament teaching salvation is expressed many times as being clothed in Christ. A clear reference to the nakedness of the Fall can be found in the words of Revelation: "I counsel you to buy from me ... and white clothes to wear, so that you can cover your shameful nakedness" (Rev 3:18). In these words of Christ to the church of Laodicea, we have been given a clear address. Clothes suitable for covering shame can be had from Jesus. Jesus himself says in the Scripture lesson on the road to Emmaus (Luke 24:25), that all Scriptures from the Law to the Prophets talk about Him. Therefore, it is natural and essential, that at the core of the covering of the

---

9 This Bible passage has sometimes been used to try to justify the inferiority and slavery of the black race. This interpretation falters already at the starting point, for though Ham can be said to be the African nations' ancestor, Canaan is, nevertheless, very clearly the ancestor of the people that lived in the Middle East.

shame is the Lord Jesus Christ. We can outline the Bible teaching of a covering cloth into different points of view:

- In baptism we are clothed into the death and resurrection of Christ (Rom 6:1–5). Christ is the garment acceptable to God, in which we can approach the holy God, just as the High Priest robed in a sacred linen tunic could enter into the Holy of Holies (Lev 16:4).
- Clothed in Christ we can have the status of a child in God's Kingdom, like the prodigal son returning home, and who was dressed in the best robes instead of rags (Luke 15:22).
- To receive the holiness of Christ is a blessed exchange; His perfect garment is taken from Him and given to us, who are under the shame of sin. He dies on the cross naked (John 19:23).
- Even our best righteousness is like filthy rags, therefore something sickening before God. Only righteousness as a gift is acceptable in front of Him. Any self-righteousness must be set aside. (Isaiah 64:6).
- The final robing will take place in connection with the resurrection of the body. Until then we are more or less naked (2 Cor 5:1–4).
- Finally, there will be a great multitude of those who are wearing white robes (Rev 7:9).

The ultimate motivation of covering is love. The praise of love that can be found in 1st Corinthians, chapter 13, describes in different ways the complete love. It is said, that although this chapter is often read in a marriage ceremony, it does not describe human love, but rather God's perfect love. However, as human love is a reflection of God's love, it is of course also fitting to read this Bible passage at a wedding. One of the verses of this chapter says love "always protects" (1 Cor 13:7). The Greek verb used here is stegō, which means to put under cover. God is love. Covering shame arises therefore from the nature of God.

Behind the atonement is covering

In the Old Testament Hebrew language, there are several words that mean the atonement of sins. One of these words is kaphar. The word kaphar literally means covering. Examples of the everyday use of the word are for example the covering of Noah's ark with ground resin. In that connection the verb kaphar is used. The word is known from the Hebrew name of Jom Kippur, the Day of Atonement. From this verb is also derived a noun kapporeth, which means the lid of the Ark of the Covenant. The lid of the Ark of the Covenant is thus literally a cover.

The thoughts of covering and atonement are so strongly linked together that when the Old Testament was translated into Greek 250 years before the birth of Christ, the name for the lid of the Ark of the Covenant was chosen to be the word hilastērion, which is derived from the verb to atone, hilaskomai. Thus, Romans 3:25 is translated in NIV that God presented Jesus as a "sacrifice of atonement". Literally this could also therefore be translated as "God made Jesus the lid of the box". From Luther's time, we have also used a beautiful explanatory translation "God made Jesus the mercy seat".

The Sanctuary is an image of God's heaven. The Ark of the Covenant describes God's throne. With the stone tablets of the Ten Commandments inside the Ark of the Covenant, and when its lid is sprinkled with the blood of the sacrificial lamb, this then presents a picture of God's holy justice and grace. Therefore, God's throne is today, in this time of grace, a throne of grace – a mercy seat. Therefore, the Book of Hebrews also says: "Let us then approach the throne of grace with confidence so that we may receive mercy and find grace to help us in our time of need" (Heb 4:16). We are therefore living in a time frame where God's holy demands are covered by the blood of Jesus.

David describes the atoning of sins in Psalm 32:1–2 through different expressions:

> *Blessed is he whose transgressions are forgiven, whose sins are covered!*
>
> *Blessed is the man whose sin the Lord does not count against him and in whose spirit is no deceit!*

The expression of *'forgiven' (nasah)* in the verse emphasises the taking away of sin and guilt. The expression of *'covered' (kasha)* in the verse refers to the covering of the shame of the sin. Removing the guilt is an easier expression for us, whereas covering the shame of the guilt speaks to representatives of the Muslim cultures. The Bible talks about both together.

Is the covering a hoax?

In the Western mind-set, the word atonement, as derived from the word covering, sounds slightly insincere. Could sin, just like that, be covered, without tackling the reasons for the problem? Would it not be wiser to strip down sin to the very end? From the point of view of guilt orientation, sin is confessed and renounced. The light of truth reveals, and then the blood cleanses. We are, from our own cultural point of view, programmed to have complete confession of the sin, before forgiveness becomes possible.

We insist that our children to say sorry to each other. Superficial apology is not good enough for us, so we demand our child to say "sorry I did this or that". In addition, we demand that you must look into the other person's eyes, when you say sorry. When from the point of view of shame, atonement is just a covering, it feels too easy for us. When the prodigal son is dressed in the best clothes, there is no mention about his undressing or washing. It is the older brother, who reveals the sinful life of the prodigal son as he accuses him of wasting the money on prostitutes.

King David's sin was revealed by the Prophet Nathan (2 Sam 12:1–14). Instead of directly blaming David for adultery, murder and robbery, he told David a poignant story. David was moved to condemn the villain of the story. Then Nathan revealed to David: "You are that man!" Nathan might have chosen this indirect way to approach the problem because it would have been fatal to accuse a king. It might be that it was more fruitful to get David to judge himself rather than to accuse him. When we are accused, we tend to start defending ourselves. In any case this was a gentler way to confront David's sin.

Within our culture David would have been required to account for his deeds in the Court of Impeachment. He would have been asked to immediately to relinquish his position. Despite the absolution declared by Nathan, it looks like David went through a considerable process with his sin. In the Psalms he prays: "Let me never be put to shame" (Ps 31:2) and asks: "Hide your face from my sins" (Ps 51:9).

Isn't the covering of shame indeed, just for this reason, a particularly merciful and gentle example of behaviour towards a sinner! A full disclosure is not required of us. God's grace hastens to cover us first before we are taken to the court room required by the culture of blame where we are accused, and where Christ is our defender. This whole drama rises from the nature of God; from the fact that He is both just and loving. His holiness demands the payment of sins and his love demands the hiding of the sinner. We are like a modern defendant who is wearing a hood to cover his face, so that greedy tabloid photographers are not able to reveal our identity. Our cover is not just any veil, but the complete holiness of Christ himself!

Humans always tend to try and hide their own shame of sin. Adam and Eve put together fig leaf skirts for themselves (Gen 3:7). The prophet Isaiah warns us by saying that self-made holiness is disgustingly dirty (Isa 64:6). Indeed, self-righteousness is repellent. Because of that believers are detested in their work places and among their relatives. God strips us from hypocrisy through a lifelong process of hardship and trials. At the end of our lives we are stripped, so that there will be nothing else left, apart from Christ.

The dress code

In the Gospel of Matthew there is a parable of the wedding of a king's son. And Jesus started once again to talk in parables and said:

> *The Kingdom of Heaven is like a king who prepared a banquet for his son. He sent his servants to those who had been invited to the banquet to tell them to come, but they refused to come. The he sent some more servants and said: 'tell those who have been invited that I have prepared my dinner: My oxen and fattened cattle have been slaughtered, and everything is ready. Come to the wedding banquet.' But they paid no attention and went off – one to his field, another to his business. The rest seized his servants, ill-treated them and killed them.*
>
> *The king was enraged. He sent his army and destroyed those murderers and burned their city. Then he said to his servants: 'The wedding banquet is ready, but those I invited did not deserve to come. Go to the street corners and invite to the banquet anyone you find.' So the servants went out into the streets and gathered all the people they could find, both good and bad and the wedding hall was filled with guests.*
>
> *But when the king came in to see the guests, he noticed a man there who was not wearing wedding clothes. 'Friend', he asked, 'how did you get in here without wedding clothes?' The man was speechless. Then the king told the attendants, 'Tie him hand and foot, and throw him outside, into the darkness, where there will be weeping and gnashing of teeth.' "For many are invited, but few are chosen."*
>
> *Then the Pharisees went out and laid plans to trap him in his words.* (Matt 22:2–15)

Generally, we only read the first part of this parable and use it for motivation for evangelistic ministry. We have to invite all and sundry into God's kingdom. We might be left confused that, those who were originally invited did not deign to come, but we understand this to describe how the well-off of society often reject the church. This is therefore an excellent text to justify all kinds of work done amongst the down and outs. Then the end of the parable gives us, however, a blow in the face. In the king's son's wedding, there was someone who was not appropriately dressed, and the angry king throws him into the darkness.

A picture is shaping into our mind of a down and out in a Western society, who just a moment earlier has been invited to a great feast, and now, suddenly he, in his rags, is not good enough for the host of the feast. What an earth is happening! The end of the parable is completely unsuitable for our use. And, we are starting to wonder, if the ending of the parable has been taken from somewhere else and just glued onto the end of this one. Or could it be that we have used this Bible passage in the wrong way? Jesus did not use this parable to enlist people into an evangelistic campaign. He told this parable as a warning to the Pharisees. The Pharisees were naturally amongst those invited but had rejected the wedding invitation. The Pharisees are therefore also those, who try to enter the wedding hall dressed inappropriately.

To understand the point of this parable, we will need to make use of a cultural key. That is to say, in Jewish weddings, it was customary for the wedding host to offer their guests simple linen wedding garments. Thus, we can understand that the king, looking around the banqueting hall, notices immediately any person, to whom the garment offered by the wedding host was not good enough. There was one was dressed in his own clothes.

There is no reason to think that the beggar, invited at the last minute, would have declined the offered wedding garment. Of course, the person declining the offer of a wedding garment by the host must have been the one who thinks his own garment, perhaps made from beautiful red silk, is so much better. The Scribes, particularly, were those who had convinced themselves that they would get to God's kingdom through their own piousness. The actual point of this parable of Jesus is that self-righteous people will be ejected from the heavenly wedding.

Dressing is a difficult matter. Sometimes we notice that we have overdressed, other times under-dressed. Various uniforms free us from worrying about a suitable costume. A conscript does not need to ponder in the morning what to wear. The order comes from his superior. Even a city bus driver has no worries when going to work. Therefore, according to the parable of Jesus, we go to God's heaven in a particular uniform.

For men dressing up is still fairly easy. When a couple goes to a festive occasion, the man wears a shirt, a suit and chooses a tie. There are not really so many options, and so he is quickly ready to go. The woman remains helpless in front of a full wardrobe and lets out a sigh: "I have nothing to wear!" That sentence, familiar in so many homes is, for a man completely unfathomable. In that sentence, however, is hidden a deep wisdom. I imagine that Adam and Eve's fig leave costumes were Adam's invention, but Eve might not have been so happy with them. Our own personal covers are not enough to cover our shame of guilt. Perhaps Eve falls in love with the handsome costumes designed by God.

In the collective memory of womanhood, there remains a strong feeling of inadequacy of one's own clothing. Even in fashion shows there is a constant search for a perfect costume, however, it still has not been found. A woman does not, of course, claim that her wardrobe is empty, but that there is nothing to wear that would completely fit the particular occasion; there are so many nuances that one must take note of: suitability with regard to the weather, season, travel to the occasion, the level of solemnity of the festivity, regarding the way others will be dressed, possible performance...

The obsession of covering

In the Islamic world women dress up magnificently amongst other women and at home. In public the search for a perfect clothing concentrates mainly on covering. The demand for cover varies according to time and place.

Looking at old photographs from the 1950s, for example from Iraq and Afghanistan, we see women who are more or less dressed in Western clothes of that period. In old photographs from Indonesia, women are dressed in traditional national costumes.

This has changed. The worldwide Islamic dress code has tightened. In these years women's dress code in Turkey has been tightened so that women have started to wear a veil. In immigrant families, women in the Western world are covered with a veil even more strictly than in their home country, because it is perceived that there are more dangers in the West.

In Saudi Arabia women's dress code is controlled and has become strict up to ever more incomprehensible extremes. Instead of being horrified of women's veiling in Islam, we can agree with the basic thought about the need to cover. Covering is honourable and revealing is shameful. This we can agree with, and therefore we must support covering.

In some churches, there is a demand for a woman who is converting to Christianity, to give up wearing a veil, before she can be baptised. I disagree with this practice. Paul teaches in his letter to the Corinthians, that women covering their heads is a sign of humility. In old Middle East churches women still cover their heads in services. This same practice continues, for example in traditional Baptist churches in Russia. If we demand giving up the veil, we place ourselves on the side of shame and disgrace. We must not make wearing the veil into a moral absolute, but rather carefully consider, what kind of a cultural message we are sending with our instructions.

So, now we can together with a Muslim bemoan the revealing Western way of dressing and ponder, what a sufficient cover would be. In pondering this, we must not content ourselves with any compromises, but we must persevere.

In the Bible a devout young man, comes to Lord Jesus and asks what more still he should do in order to gain the eternal life. He believed he had already fulfilled all the commandments. Jesus is not satisfied with this but demands even more. This could be described thus: the young man had climbed to the top of the mountain towards God and asks, is this enough. Jesus does not criticise him over his climbing, but encourages him to jump another 10 meters higher up from the top of the mountain. The young man has run out of means. In the same way, we could use the need to cover as a sermon of the law. The essential thing is, that we are on the same side with the Muslim, but that we show that her or his covering is not enough.[10]

Only perfect clothing may cover sufficiently. Just as the clothing was provided for the guests in the wedding feast of the king's son, so we too have to receive this perfect clothing as a gift. God has provided a perfect cover, just as he indicated already in the garden of Eden. God had the plan for covering from the very beginning. He expressed his good will immediately after Adam's sin. In the account of crucifixion, we are told that Jesus was wearing a seamless undergarment. He was clothed in a carefully manufactured, highly expensive underwear.

We can, therefore, state that Jesus did not go about in cheap clothing. His outfit is precious and complete. He gave up that complete cover for our sakes and placed himself under public shame. We, who are under the shame of sin and naked, may clothe ourselves in His sinlessness and complete holiness. Jesus Christ is the only sufficient garment.

Our shame offends God

The honour and shame in regard to dress always lie in relation to society. Nobody dresses only for himself, but also for the eyes of the others. The way we dress may bring disgrace, apart from to ourselves, to the host of the feast or to our family. In the Biblical language of instruction, the woman is the glory of the husband, and the son of his father. For a Muslim this is important, but for us Westerners this is a lot to swallow. Every man, however, recognises in himself the feeling that he does not want his wife to dress in such a way as to let other men eye her too closely. All parents recognise in themselves the pride of their children's school success. The essential part of

---

[10] The reader might stop here to ponder whether it is right to demand endless covering, even though it still is not our final purpose and opinion. We can also pose the question like this: Is it right to use the Islamic law to awaken contrition? Paul teaches that our human-made rules are enough to show that a person is under judgement but cannot save himself. The sermon of the law can therefore be declared on the grounds of other laws, not just God's laws. Why not then base it even on the Islamic dress code!

a man's 50th birthday celebration is that his children are present at the party, and thus honour their father.

The radical claim in the Bible is that we shame God by our sins. "...you dishonour God by breaking the law" (Rom 2:23). Islam categorically denies this Bible teaching. According to Islam God is absolutely impervious to our sins. God is greater, is the Muslim war cry, which we hear in Arabic words "Allahu akbar". Sin cannot have any effect on God, Muslims say emphatically.

One of Job's advisors suggests a similar Islamic-sounding teaching:

> *Then Elihu said: "Do you think this is just? You say, 'I shall be cleared by God.' Yet you ask him, 'What profit is it to me, and what do I gain by not sinning.' I would like to reply to you and to your friends with you. Look up at the heavens and see; gaze at the clouds so high above you. If your sins are many, what does that do to him? If you are righteous, what do you give to him, or what does he receive from your hand? Your wickedness affects only a man like yourself and your righteousness only the sons of men."* (Job 35:1–8)

We must be careful when reading the book of Job. Job's friends' advice includes something true and right but yet mixed it with untruths. It is true, that God is almighty and beyond our reach. But God has set Himself near us and He places Himself on the cross to be wounded by our sins.

Family honour

We can approach this matter from the point of view of internal family honour. In the same way, that a child can harm his father's honour, we can harm God's honour with our sins. The Muslim culture of honour is in fact, closer to the Biblical family culture than our Western culture in which parents give their children freedom to decide for themselves. We think that a mother should not interfere with her daughter's marriage and a father should not be offended if his son fools about in town; that is the children's own business.

In the instructions concerning the laws of Moses in the Bible, a son who shames his parents deserves the death penalty (Deut 21:18–21). The Mosaic instructions of the law were part of the law of the nation of Israel. And they should not, as they are, be transferred into the Christian thinking of legislation. Behind this statute is, however, a commandment which concerns also Christians: "honour your father and mother". This Bible passage which talks about a disobedient son, continues in an odd way when it talks about the death penalty and curse of the one who committed the offense. The one hung on a tree is declared cursed (Deut 21:22–23). Paul picks up this detail in his letter (Gal 3:13) and applies it to the death on the cross of our Lord Jesus.

Keeping in mind this thought we will now examine the story of a particular incident. An Iraqi young man was in court accused of threatening behaviour. He had threatened to kill his sister. The sister had arrived in Finland a few years earlier and settled well into life here. Perhaps even too well, as the Iraqi community had started to talk about her lifestyle. Soon the rumours reached Iraq and her father's ears. The disgraced father seethed with anger, when he heard that his daughter was meeting with an infidel man. Due to the daughter's lifestyle, the family ended up being subjected to mocking and shame. The heaviest shame lay on the father's shoulders.

Finally, the father assigned a heavy task to his oldest son: "You must go to that faraway country and kill your sister, who shames our whole family." The dutiful son set off on his journey and after finding his sister told her about the task given to him. The girl had learnt something about life in the west, and rang the police immediately, at which point the stunned brother was arrested. Following the advice of his solicitor the brother told the court that he was not really going to kill his sister, but had just used strong language. He managed to get off with a fine, before he was deported.

Honour killing and the role of Jesus

Instead of being horrified about this honour killing that nearly happened, I will invite us now to empathise with the lost honour of the father. If we are able to think about the incident through the culture of shame, this opens up an excellent frame for a story to share the Gospel. We humans are like the daughter, who had brought shame to his father. We have disgraced God with our sins. What does God do in this situation? He sends his son to us. The surprise in the story is shown in that God does not send his son to kill us. For God did not send his Son into the world to condemn the world, but to save it through him (John 3:17). God's Son did not come to judge, but to die himself for us.

The logic of an honour killing is in that the problem is not guilt but shame. In this thinking the family might in an extreme situation kill the daughter that was raped. The reason for killing the daughter is not, fundamentally, because she would be blamed for carelessness. The culprit will not even be searched for because the problem is not guilt, but shame. The shame is identified through the daughter. When the family has killed the blameless victim, the shame has been removed: it is no longer possible to see the daughter whose presence brings to mind the shameful deed, and thus public shame is avoided. All is fine again. We can try to understand this thinking, but I am not suggesting that we should accept it. Neither does the Bible accept it. The answer from the Gospel to the question of shame is Jesus Christ, who, to our surprise carries our shame and dies a shameful death on the cross.

The Son of God gave up his glory and radiance and chose shame. God does not remove the shame but takes it on himself. Instead, we are clothed in glory that does not belong to us. The Muslims are correct: the cross is an insult. The cross is too shameful. The shame of the cross should shake us to the core. Precisely for that reason the message of the cross is so powerful amongst the Muslims. Therefore, we also must, risking everything, declare the message of the cross of Jesus the Messiah to Muslims.

THE COMMUNITY OF HONOUR AND SHAME

The individuals in a Community

The dynamics of honour and shame do not work in a culture which is centred on an individual. Shame and honour mean something only if there is a family and an extended family structure. For people in a culture which has become psychologised and self-centred, shame is like a meaningless and malignant appendix. In the Western reality, the basic structures of the society are well on the way to disintegrate. Therefore, we are approaching a time of ultimate shamelessness. We can hope that with the increase of Islamic influence in our societies at least something of the sense of a community could be recovered.

Christian churches should be islands of communality within the climate of individualisation. Any communal influence on an individual's values can, however, be seen as mental violence. Our society cannot stand the moral rules set by the Evangelical churches for their members, or those of a youth worker for youngsters with regard to dating for example. We have lost our natural ability to see the difference between a healthy sense of community and mental violence. The community offers secure safety, but the same safety walls also limit an individual's freedom.

In the Bible, the background of any incident is always within and part of a communal culture. Let us consider one such incident and examine how honour and shame define people.

> *When Jesus had again crossed over by boat to the other side of the lake, a large crowd gathered around him while he was by the lake Then one of the synagogue rulers, named Jairus, came there. Seeing Jesus, he fell at his feet and pleaded earnestly with him, "My little daughter is dying. Please come and put your hands on her so that she will be healed and live." So, Jesus went with him. A large crowd followed and pressed around him.*
>
> *And a woman was there who had been subject to bleeding for twelve years. She had suffered a great deal under the care of many doctors and had spent all she had, yet instead of getting better she grew worse. When she heard about Jesus, she came up behind him in the crowd and touched his cloak, because she thought "If I just touch his clothes, I will be healed."*
>
> *Immediately her bleeding stopped and she felt in her body that she was freed from her suffering. At once Jesus realised that power had gone out from him. He turned around in the crowd and asked, "Who touched my clothes?"*

> *"You see people crowding against you," his disciples answered, "and yet you can ask, 'Who touched me?'" But he kept looking around to see who had done it. Then the woman knowing what had happened to her, came and fell at his feet and, trembling with feat, told him the whole truth. He said to her, "Daughter, your faith has healed you. Go in peace and be freed from your suffering."*
>
> *While Jesus was still speaking, some men came from the house of Jairus, the synagogue ruler. "Your daughter is dead," they said. "Why bother the teacher anymore?" Ignoring what they said, Jesus told the synagogue ruler, "Don't be afraid; just believe." He did not let anyone follow him except Peter, James and John the brother of James. When they came to the home of the synagogue ruler, Jesus saw a commotion, with people crying and wailing loudly. He went in and said to them "Why all this commotion and wailing? The child is not dead but asleep." But they laughed at him.*
>
> *After he put them all out, he took the child's father and mother and the disciples who were with him and went in where the child was. He took her by the hand and said to her, "Talitha koum!" (which means, "Little girl, I say to you, get up!") Immediately the girl stood up and walked around (she was twelve years old). At this they were completely astonished. He gave strict order not to let anyone know about this, and told them to give her something to eat.* (Mark 5:21–43, see also Luke 8:40–56)

In Christian churches, we count up statistics and estimate ministry numerically. We hope for large attendance at our services. Jesus never seemed to be interested in huge crowds. He meets individuals. Jesus seems to break the communal cultural pattern with his appreciation of an individual person. We might even insist that Jesus, with his actions and attitude, sets the basics for the declaration of human rights, and the Western thinking that emphasises individual freedom. However, contrary to Western culture, Jesus also considers the individual's relationship with the community. In this Bible passage Jesus meets a respected synagogue leader and a woman pushed aside by the community. We will now further examine these characters.

Clean motives?

The immigration offices of European states carefully interview those asylum seekers who have become Christians. They are examined as individuals. It looks like the main aim is to clarify whether the asylum seeker has gone through an authentic and deep conversion experience in his private world of emotional values. This is bizarre, for from the point of view of the government it can hardly be of huge significance how authentic Christians new immigrants are. From the point of view of the secular court the most relevant issue should be to clarify the convert's status in the society from which he became a Christian. The Muslim community is not interested in how authentic or with what motives a Muslim community member becomes a Christian. The demand to kill an apostate is there, however, whether he believed in Jesus from his whole heart or whether he was just a Christian in name. Renouncing the Islamic faith is the highest defamation against the whole Islamic society. The secular society should defend freedom of belief, which also includes the right to become a Christian or a Muslim in name only.

In fact, people very seldom, if ever, become Christians out of completely pure motives. Even in the Gospel stories people didn't turn to Jesus with pure motives. They were more or less all pursuing their own interest. Excellent examples of this are the synagogue leader from the above Bible passage and the woman suffering from bleeding. Was the synagogue leader really going to become a disciple of Jesus? Absolutely not! Was Jesus the first option of the woman suffering with the bleeding? Indeed not. The woman had already had time to try other options that she thought were better. Jesus came only after the so-called better solution options had failed. The woman had already managed to use up all her possessions and had suffered a lot at the hands of many a doctor. (An amusing detail is that Luke himself a doctor, carefully remarks that the previous doctors had done their best).

So, if the people met by Jesus were not genuine followers, how can we then imagine that we could sift through for baptism only those who are authentic followers of Jesus? Which one of us is a follower with completely altruistic motives?

The bearers of the honour and shame

In this Bible passage we are presented with two miracles of Jesus that are related. These two miracles take place, determined by the scale of honour and shame, at each extreme of society. One is a religious leader and the other is an unclean person. Note, that there is no mention of sin or guilt of either person. Due to the bleeding the woman is ritually unclean. Therefore, she has been cut off from society. It is shame defines this woman's status in the society. In the same way the man in the story is defined by his honorary status in the community. Being the leader of a synagogue is not a profession which you reach based on your professional ability; it is an honorary position for which a person who enjoys the confidence and trust of the society was chosen.

On that day in the ministry of our Lord Jesus Christ, the fates of a central community leader and a person pushed to the edge of the community were entwined together.

The synagogue leader is presented to us by name. This respected person, Jairus, is the father of a small girl. His daughter is close to death. His daughter urgently needs help. When he heard that the rabbi who heals was in town, Jairus decides to risk his social standing. Jesus was a controversial person. It was not politically wise to side with Jesus. However, because of his daughter he throws himself down at the feet of Jesus to beg for help. The crowd construed this to mean that he had thus publicly acknowledged Jesus' status. This might cost him his whole honourable standing in the society. The social status achieved by his whole extended family was at risk. Jairus was, however, prepared to lose that for generations to come because of his daughter.

All Muslims come from one or another step in their societal hierarchy of honour. For all of them accepting Jesus would mean losing everything in their society. When the most honoured people in a Muslim society turn to Christ, there is a lot at stake. It was the same way in the Jewish society. When Jesus discusses with Nicodemus, the same elements are present as would be when talking with an honoured Muslim. Nicodemus hides his interest in critical religious debate.

In that debate The Lord Jesus gives us the most glorious definitions of the Gospel and the famous mini gospel: "For God so loved the world that he gave his one and only Son that whoever believes in him shall not perish but have eternal life." (John 3:16). Jesus strongly invites Nicodemus to publicly acknowledge his faith and thus to become his follower.

Jairus is brave in his confession. Generally, we are told that believers started to follow Jesus – now we are told that Jesus started to follow Jairus towards his house. We can be comforted by the fact, that Jesus is guided to go because of Jairus' need. We can imagine that in the same way he will direct his steps towards our need. But then, something peculiar happens: another person's need captures the attention of Jesus. When he lived as a human being on earth, Jesus could only be in one place at once. Jesus now had to choose his priorities between Jairus and the woman.

The woman with the bleeding was introduced to us without a name. Perhaps the evangelists did not want to remind the readers of this woman's shameful history. The woman and her relatives were still present amongst the readers (or listeners), so nobody wanted to sully their reputation with something from the past. We could think that unlike Jairus, this woman had nothing to lose. That was not quite the case. The woman, because of her impurity had been condemned to be outside society. She could not come to the temple. Everyone who ended up in contact with her also became unclean for a certain time.

When the woman broke the inviolability order, she could expect an angry reaction from the crowd. She is justly scared when it appears that she had secretly, from behind, touched the cloak of Jesus. Due to her shame the woman was in danger of losing her life. In the same way as that woman, the most despised members of the Muslim communities may be more open to the Gospel, but it does not mean that they would be safe when turning to Jesus.

Both of them, Jairus and the woman wanted help from Jesus without people noticing. With both of them, Jesus compels them to a public acknowledgment. With Jairus that would mean falling from his own pedestal of honour. When the woman is already healed, Jesus stops and asks who touched Him. Jesus reveals the woman – not to put her under shame, but to show the crowd that the woman's shame has been removed. Jesus heals the illness and also saves her from shame.

Jesus gives the shamed priority

Both, the woman and Jairus won the favour of Jesus, but the woman cut in before Jairus. According to the culture of honour Jesus should have understood that the need of Jairus was more valuable than that of the woman. According to Western thinking Jairus had reserved a meeting with Jesus first and the woman should have quietly waited in the queue for her own turn. According to the urgency of the need, the dying daughter was an emergency, whereas the woman had already had the ailment for 12 years. Her need was not so urgent. Yet, Jesus deals with the woman's need first.

In the Eastern culture matters are not judged according to their urgency but by social importance. Jesus deems it important to elevate this woman to high regard within a culture of honour and shame. Therefore Jesus, to everyone's amazement stops to encounter this woman. In so doing He shook the customary perceptions of honour.

We can only surmise how Jairus might feel about this injustice and shame towards himself. He might have tried to hurry Jesus to continue the journey. Perhaps Jesus was often late – in our opinion. Even as regards Lazarus' healing He was late. I must admit that I would have torn my hair out many times, if I had had to work as Jesus' secretary or driver. At Jairus' house I would have snapped at Him: "Look! Was it worth spending time with that insignificant woman? By now the daughter of the most important person in the society must have died. How could you be late!"

When Jesus arrived at the house, he does not apologise. He does not even give a word of comfort. He merely curtly states that the girl is just sleeping. Sleeping is not some Hebrew euphemism for dying. According to the reaction of the people, it was an odd expression. However, Jesus used this expression repeatedly. It was his understanding of the power of death. Jesus understated the power of death as if being defiant before a great battle. Due to the victory of Jesus, death has indeed become to us like a night of sleep which starts in the evening when we close our eyes, and finishes immediately when we hear the alarm go off in the morning.

Death becomes insignificant and short, when we think that Jesus will raise us up from death on the last day. The disciples remember, still many years later, the moment, when Jesus said these words to the girl: "Talitha Koum", little girl rise up. Therefore, these words are repeated in Aramean in the Gospel. It is not a question of any magic words, but of a clear recollection. After waking up, the first person the girl sees is Jesus. This is our resurrection! We also, can see our dear Lord Jesus after we wake up from our sleep of death.

Saved into the community of grace

Jesus Christ hated the power of sin in this world. When He encountered the power of sin in the woman's illness or in Jairus' daughter, He wanted to fight the powers of destruction. According to the established Jewish thinking, any person would have become unclean if a person with this disease had touched him, or if he had come into contact with a dead person.

But In the case of Jesus, these consequences are different. The filth does not transfer onto Jesus, but the greater holiness of Jesus will transfer onto these two, healing them from the effects of death and ritual uncleanness.

An excellent example of a conversion of a disgraced person to become a follower of Jesus is the woman at the well of the town of Sychar. Like the woman with the bleeding, this woman also is alone and ostracised by the community. They are both persons, who badly needed the acceptance of their community, at the same time as they shun its attention. The woman of Sychar becomes the trendsetter for her town. The community does not shun her anymore but follows her to Jesus.

We can classify the people Jesus met into two groups: religious experts, with whom Lord Jesus held debates that ended in disagreements, and social outcasts, who unconditionally trust in Jesus in their need. Only on rare occasions do those with religious authority relate to Jesus with trust, such as Jairus here. Only rarely do the disgraced of the society reject Jesus. Jesus is open to both, but at the same time he disturbs the standing of both in the society's scale of honour. By his own actions Jesus dismantles those at the top of the society of their honour while gently covering those under shame with his own glory. We note that Jesus does not reject or evade the social shame-honour hierarchy, but this hierarchy is a fundamental sphere of action for him. He is using the shame-honour culture to communicate his message.

In Jesus' ministry God's Kingdom breaks through. God's Kingdom is not just miracles and forgiveness of sins. God's Kingdom introduces God's community right here in our midst In this human community. In God's community none of the earned value hierarchies are valid, rather this is a community of grace. In this community, we are not measured by the respect afforded to each other, as in a community of shame, where everyone competes for a limited amount of honour. In God's Kingdom, we have a relationship with Jesus and receive for ourselves unlimited honour, because we are partakers of Christ's glory and honour. In God's Kingdom honour does not lessen, when we place our brothers and sisters above ourselves.

THE FATHER WHO RELINQUISHED HIS HONOUR

This story truly carries away

The story of the prodigal son is truly a pearl of world literature. In this parable, which I quote in its entirety after a couple pages, there are enough fascinating details and layers of meaning for untold sermons and books. The unbelievable depth of the account offers us again and again new views. It is worthwhile to dive into the worlds of this familiar parable from the point of view of the communal culture of shame.

Used as a way of approach, Bible stories communicate feelings, attitudes and major principles effectively. Doctrinal definitions are useful and exact in a situation where the meanings of individual words are carefully defined. In a Bible translation into a new language stories offer a more precise understanding compared to short doctrinal statements.

The Bible stories may look to today's reader as scanty and frugal, however, compared to other literature from the same period, they are plentiful: containing a lot of juicy details and dramatics. Part of the dramatics of the story of the prodigal son opens up only when we look at it from the cultural point of view, as Kenneth Bailey in his books "Finding the lost" and "Jacob & the Prodigal" has in an excellent way shown.[11]

In Middle East villages, old men relate stories around the evening camp fire. The elders of the community still remember the time before television, when evenings were spent listening to the same stories over and over again, and thus they were learnt by heart word for word. I have interviewed old men, who remember that time with nostalgia. Part of the fascination of a story is particularly the fact that, apart from the youngest ones, everyone knows how the story goes, and admires the narration skills of the storyteller. At the same time the listeners, as they get older, prepare themselves one day to be in storyteller's role.

As a young missionary, I learnt that a good story must always have a moral. I remember how I tried to tell a joke to people from the Muslim culture. My friends laughed politely at my joke, when I myself first laughed giving them a signal. There followed, however, a moment of silence, after which I was

---

[11] Kenneth E. Bailey, Finding the Lost: Cultural Keys to Luke 15, Concordia Publishing House, 1992) and Kenneth E: Bailey, Jacob & and the Prodigal. How Jesus retold Israel's Story, InterVarsity Press, 2003).

presented a question: “Could you repeat what the teaching of this story was.” Hastily I made up some wisdom for my joke and decided that from now on I will concentrate on stories with a lesson to learn, not, of course forgetting the humour.

The shame bearer is abandoned outside the family

The central tension in the Prodigal Son story is in the father-son relationship and the related demand for respect. We find ourselves facing again the question of shame and honour through the internal relationships and values in the family. In the Islamic culture the father’s honourable status is undisputed. The children must respect their parents and this expression of respect accumulates to the father’s “honour bank”. If the child brings shame upon his father, the father might even disown him or her. I used to be friends with a young man, who had run away from home in order to avoid an arranged marriage. When he rang home to his mother, the father snatched the phone from the mother and shouted: “You are not my son anymore!” He had become an orphan, because he had shamed his father in front of his family.

Many of those who have become Christians from a Muslim background have ended up being disowned by their family. Ending up outside the family means being without an inheritance and perhaps also losing one’s family name. Losing a social network also means that there is no more social protection within the family, such as a home, a job or perhaps a study place gained through family relationships. The heaviest loss is, however, the fact that the one who has become a Christian cannot have a spouse, and is often left deserted and without heirs.

One can disgrace parents in many ways, but abandoning the religion of Islam is the heaviest shame to the parents. Another extremely heavy burden is if the child refuses the already arranged marriage. At that point the parents will become marked by shame in front of the whole extended family community. In a situation like this, the father often renounces his son or daughter. The child simply just does not exist anymore for the community.

The prodigal son despises his father

Against all this background the prodigal son’s behaviour towards his father is something unheard of. It may be that the father disowns a son, but that the son would disown the father – that is unthinkable. In this story the son, when asking for his inheritance, is in practice he renouncing his father. It is as if the son said: “Father, although you are still alive, could we imagine that you were already dead?” The setting of this story is so shocking, that a person from a Muslim background becomes angry already at hearing the first sentences and demands that the son be killed. Now that we have taken the stand of despising the son, let us read the whole story.

> *Jesus continued: "There was a man who had two sons. The younger one said to his father, 'Father, give me my share of the estate.' So, he divided his property between them." Not long after that, the young son got together all he had, set off for a distant country and there squandered his wealth in wild living. After he had spent everything, there was a severe famine in that country, and he began to be in need. So, he went and hired himself out to the citizen of that country, who sent him to his fields to feed the pigs. He longed to fill his stomach with the pods that the pigs were eating, but no-one gave him anything. "When he came to his senses, he said, 'How many of my father's hired men have food to spare, and here I am starving to death! I will set out and go back to my father and say to him: Father, I have sinned against heaven and against you. I am no longer worthy to be called your son; make me like one of your hired men.' So, he got up and went to his father. "But while he was still a long way off, his father saw him and was filled with compassion for him; he ran to his son, threw his arms around him and kissed him. "The son said to him, 'Father, I have sinned against heaven and against you. I am no longer worthy to be called your son.' "But the father said to his servants, 'Quick! Bring the best robe and put it on him. Put a ring on his finger and sandals on his feet. Bring the fattened calf and kill it. Let's have a feast and celebrate. For this son of mine was dead and is alive again; he was lost and is found.' So, they began to celebrate. "Meanwhile, the older son was in the field. When he came near the house, he heard music and dancing. So, he called one of the servants and asked him what was going on. 'Your brother has come', he replied, 'and your father has killed the fattened calf because he has him back safe and sound.' The older brother became very angry and refused to go in. So, his father went out and pleaded with him. But he answered his father, 'Look! All these years I've been slaving for you and never disobeyed your orders. Yet you never gave even a young goat so I could celebrate with my friends. But when this son of yours who had squandered your property with prostitutes comes home, you kill the fattened calf for him!' "'My son,' the father said, 'you are always with me, and everything I have is yours. But we had to celebrate and be glad, because this brother of yours was dead and is alive again; he was lost and is found.'"* (Luke 15:1–32)

The father does not die – the son dies

Despite the prodigal son's hopes for an inheritance, his father of course, does not die. In fact, the son dies. Jesus chooses his expression carefully and twice puts words into the father's mouth according to which the son died – not just "we thought he was dead", but "my son was dead". When a person declares his independence from God, or even that God does not exist, then God does not die, but the person does. In the garden of Eden God warned Adam not to eat the fruit of the forbidden tree, saying that on the day you eat it, you will surely die. Adam did not immediately die physically – he lost communion with God, and so Adam died spiritually. We see this too as an illustration, when the prodigal son dies he is separated from his father. He is not a son anymore, but a stranger and alien. In fact, spiritual death is a much more serious death than physical death. Perhaps that is the reason why God, in the garden, used that superlative form – 'die-die', as it is literally expressed in the Hebrew language (Gen 2:17).

Adam is the first prodigal son. He wanted everything immediately. He wanted to be like God. The Bible uses the expression "will understand like God". This does not mean that God would be against understanding or that He would even want to limit the knowledge of man. On the contrary, God particularly encouraged Adam to name and thus categorise the animals. We can see here the beginnings of natural science. God created man in his image also in a sense that as He is all-knowing, the man would also like to know everything. Jesus talks about knowledge and understanding always in a positive tone. We ought then to search for an answer to the question in which way "knowing like God" is harmful. I believe the point is that man did not want to accept God's definition of good and evil, but he himself wanted to decide what is right and wrong. The issue is man's "I do know" attitude. That which God had particularly stated to be "forbidden", man said was "good". According to man's assessment "... the fruit of the tree was good for food and pleasing to the eye, and also desirable for gaining wisdom" (Gen 3:6). Knowledge, when separated from God, is distorted knowledge.

The caliph replacing the caliph

As Adam wanted to be like God, he reached upwards, but in fact the result was a fall, i.e. falling down. Man's status truly collapsed. God had set man to rule and govern the creation, including birds and fish. Adam had a much wider authority than just being over domestic animals. He was the lord of the whole creation. He was the heir of paradise.

In the Islamic world the ruler is called a caliph. They understand that Adam was the first caliph. His caliphate was undisputed and perfect. Adam, however, made a mistake and lost the position as the caliph. Satan wanted to be the caliph and managed to con man out of that role. In the Bible Jesus calls Satan "the prince of this world" (John 12:31). The expression does not give Satan the right for this position. He continues to be just an outlaw prince whose power is usurped power.

In the Quran, there is a story borrowed from Jewish stories about the fall of Satan. According to the account, in the beginning God brought his angels to bow down to Adam one by one. One of the angels refused to humble himself and remarked to God how much trouble and disappointment man would cause (Quran 7:11, 17). This disobedient angel thus became a fallen angel, Satan. The Bible confirms the thought that the angels are serving spirits (Heb 1:14). The Bible also confirms that in the end all, even the fallen angels, must bow down to Jesus Christ, who is man and God (Eph 1:20–21; Heb 1:6).[12]

Islam does not acknowledge the teaching of original sin in the sense that guilt would be passed down to children from their parents. Islam does, however acknowledge the fundamental issue that Adam lost paradise, and that from thereon all people are born outside paradise. This is one of the dimensions of original sin. The lost paradise is the basic problem of the mankind. Islam aims to offer a solution for our desire to return to paradise.

Throughout its history Islam has aimed to restore paradise on earth. It is thought that a perfect Islamic nation would come nearest to being paradise. Therefore, the Islamic world became excited, when, at the time of the ISIS reign was at its most powerful, al-Baghdadi declared in Mosul's main mosque that a new caliphate has been founded. A caliph is like a new Adam who will, as a world ruler, restore the status given at the creation. Now that caliphate has collapsed just as all previous caliphates, a caliphate remains a dream vision.

The filthy rich and the pauper

We are still the children of our spendthrift father Adam, far away in a foreign country. Our inheritance is a lost inheritance – poverty. We are without a relationship to God; without the original righteousness which Adam enjoyed. According to an odd Biblical expression we are "God's offspring" (Acts 17:29; Luke 3:38) and heirs, but as prodigal children we are dead and without an inheritance. In Adam's testament there are no riches promised. Everything has been lost.

The New Testament of Jesus Christ, however, promises more. *"For if, by the trespass of the one man, death reigned through that one man, how much more, those who receive God's abundant provision of grace and the gift of*

---

[12] In Jewish (extra-Biblical) literature there is a well-known story about the fall of Satan. A book called The Life of Adam and Eve from the 1th century AD tells this story in the same way as the Quran later on. I refer to 'The Life of Adam and Eve', as translated by M. D. Johnson from the Vita manuscript, found in The Old Testament Pseudepigrapha volume II by James H. Charlesworth, p. 262. In the Quran the same story can be found briefly in sura 2, verse 34.

righteousness, will reign in the life through the one man, Jesus Christ" (Rom 5:17). God is the father of Jesus. Jesus is rich: He rightfully has all power in heaven and on earth. He therefore, has a legacy of dominion or a caliphate to leave as an inheritance.[13]

When Jesus Christ was being tempted, Satan promised Him all the domains of the world. Satan was playing his game using all his tricks. The offer was shrewd because it looked like a way to return to people all that Adam had lost at the Fall. The cost of the deal was, however, that Jesus should bow down before Satan. Thus, Satan now tried to trick Jesus to relinquish His position, just as he had earlier tricked Adam to relinquish his position. Jesus replies with the Biblical truth, worship the Lord your God only (Matt 4:10; Gen 20:2–5). Satan aspired to replace God by becoming God. Jesus did not surrender.

Beside this, it is interesting to note that the word 'Islam' means submission. The word 'Muslim' means a person, who has submitted. Islam demands bowing down again and again. A prophet of Islam declares the necessity of submission and strives to take possession of all the world's kingdoms and riches. I once witnessed an instant when a religious Muslim scholar was startled to realise that when an Islamic prophet bows down he receives all the world's kingdoms and their riches – whereas Jesus refused to bow down and refused all the power and riches of the world. This was followed by a dramatic new understanding of who Muslims in reality, bow down to. All the caliphs then in reality, are just copies of the old Adam, and similarly submit to deceit.

The Bible states that at the name of Jesus every knee shall bow in heaven, on earth and under the earth. He has been given all power in heaven and on earth. He is the legitimate Pantokrator, the Almighty king. It is not only people who will bow before him, but everything in heaven, on earth and under the earth; all people and angels (Phil 2:10; Rev 5:8). Also, Satan must finally submit and bow down to Christ. At that time Christ glorified will still continue to have a human form, in which He will be taken to heaven to the throne of God. Finally, Satan will be then forced to bow down before a man.

---

[13] The Hebrew word Bᵊrît and the Greek word Diathēkē can both be translated either as a covenant or a testament. The original word is therefore richer, and in translation, the meaning is of necessity narrower. As a rule, Bible translators have decided upon using the word covenant. Only in the letters to the Galatians and Hebrews can we find sentences where the context has demanded the use of the word 'testament'. Based on these two passages Hieronymus, when translating the Bible into Latin at the end of the 3rd century AD, ended up using the words Old Testament and New Testament to the level of headings. In some Bibles on the first pages of the New Testament this has beautifully been rendered as "The New Testament of our Lord Jesus Christ".

A speech to the father

The prodigal son, after losing his fortune, ends up being a swineherd. A pig is considered the most unclean animal within Judaism and Islam. The final straw in the prodigal son's fate was that he would have been ready to eat food meant for the pigs, but even that he was not allowed to do. He had sunk lower than the most unclean animals. He had become a servant of pigs. He, who even angels were meant to bow down to, now bows down to pigs.

In that situation, the son searched his heart, that is, he started to ponder the way his life was going. It was as if he stepped outside himself and looked at himself. Particularly he starts to compare himself to the hired help of his father and realises that he is in a considerably poorer situation. In his mind a plan starts to take shape. He prepares a speech to his father, which has three parts:

1. Father, I have sinned against heaven and against you.
2. I no longer deserve to be called your son.
3. Make me one of your hired help.

The first two points of the speech, present the problem. These points are the truth, which stop him from returning. The third sentence is crucial, because it presents the solution to his returning. The Greek word for a hired help refers to a daily hired help, whose standing is lower than for example that of a permanent slave. A hired help has no guarantees of the next day's meal. His employment is guaranteed for just one day at a time. This is the lowest position a worker can possibly have. In this situation, the worker earns favour before the master with hard work, and a possibility to continue another day. The prodigal son imagines in his mind that if he eagerly shovels muck in his father's cow shed that the father will ask his slaves: "Who is that hard working labourer there behind the cow shed? Re-employ him tomorrow as well!" Perhaps one day he might even earn a permanent position in the house.

The slave's mindset

Jesus Christ teaches us in the Gospel of John, that a slave will not remain in the house of God, because he is not an heir. So, Jesus told to the Jews who believed in him:

> *"If you hold to my teaching you are really my disciples. Then you will know the truth, and the truth will set you free. They answered him, "We are Abraham's descendants and have never been slaves of anyone. How can you say that we shall be set free?" Jesus replied, "I tell you the truth, everyone who sins is a slave to sin. Now a slave has no permanent place in*

> *the family, but a son belongs to it forever. So, if the Son sets you free, you will be free indeed. I know you are Abraham's descendants. Yet you are ready to kill me, because you have no room for my word. I am telling you what I have seen in the Father's presence, and you do what you have heard from your father." "Abraham is our father," they answered: "If you were Abraham's children," said Jesus, "then you would do the things Abraham did. As it is, you are determined to kill me, a man who has told you the truth that I heard from God. Abraham did not do such things. You are doing the things your own father does." "We are not illegitimate children," they protested. "The only Father we have is God himself." Jesus said to them, "If God were your Father, you would love me, for I came from God and now am here. I have not come on my own; but he sent me. Why is my language not clear to you? Because you are unable to hear what I say. You belong to your father, the devil, and you want to carry out your father's desire. He was a murderer from the beginning, not holding to the truth, for there is no truth in him. When he lies, he speaks his native language, for he is a liar and the father of lies. Yet because I tell the truth, you do not believe me! Can any of you prove me guilty of sin? If I am telling the truth, why don't you believe me? He who belongs to God hears what God says. The reason you do not hear is that you do not belong to God. The Jews answered him, "Aren't we right in saying that you are a Samaritan and demon-possessed?" "I am not possessed by a demon," said Jesus, "but I honour my Father and you dishonour me. I am not seeking glory for myself; but there is one who seeks it, and he is the judge.* (John 8:31–50).

In the attitude of a slave there must be something deeply offensive to God.

It is good to notice that even this conversation is being held with people who have taken a religious stand. The basic condition of a person is slavery with regard to sin and devil. On top of this a religious person transfers the pattern of slavery into his relationship with God. This was the problem that Jesus repeatedly points out to the Pharisees and scribes. On a larger scale this is the problem of all religiousness, whether Hinduism, Christianity or any other religion. Man strives to be good enough for God with his own good deeds, religious achievements or by punishing himself.

When the Jews said they were Abraham's descendants, Jesus disputes this, because being a descendant of Abraham would mean trusting the promise, instead of one's own attempts. When the Jews call God their father, Jesus denies this even more emphatically, and tells them they are from the devil himself. These are perhaps the harshest words of Jesus that the Gospels have recorded for us. In the attitude of a slave there must therefore be something deeply offensive to God.

The prodigal son had assumed the mind of a slave. God did not plan for us to be slaves but rather to have the status of a prince. Through the Fall, however, man ended up being a slave to sin and to Satan. The model of slavery has eaten so deeply into our fallen hearts that we bring it out in our relationship with God. The mind of a slave does not, however, belong to our relationship with God. *"For you did not receive a spirit that makes you a slave again to fear, but you received the Spirit of sonship. And by him we cry, 'Abba! Father.'"* (Rom 8:15). God wants children for himself, not slaves. *"Yet to all who received him, to those who believed in his name, he gave the right to become children of God"* (John 1:12.

In fact, the plan of the prodigal son is extremely shameful. First, the fact that he dares to think he can just return to his father's village after offending him so deeply, is already a huge offence. Everyone from the Middle East would understand to stay away from the sight of the father after such an insult. To the horror of a Muslim reader this son, however, dares to plan to return to his own neighbourhood. Even more abhorrent is his plan to earn his father's acceptance. He continues to think that his father's acceptance is so cheap, that he, with his work, could buy his father's respect. We can compare this to a son who digs out a few notes from his purse, hands them over to his father and in this way offers to pay for the father's love. Every father would understand that he had been mortally offended.

A person from the Islamic cultural background realises that the prodigal son's plan is extremely repulsive for the father. Islam, however, offers precisely this approach back to God: a Muslim has a precarious status of a slave, in which one can possibly earn God's favour through religious performance. One of the most favourite Islamic names, which also was Muhammed's father's name, is Abdullah, which means God's slave.

The Islamic ideal is slavery in relation to God. Slavery is practised through religious obligations: prayer performance, reciting the creed, fasting, alms and the hajj. All these are considered virtuous deeds. How deeply does this religious slavery offend God! How cheaply does it treat God's honour! How easily does even a Christian imagine achieving God's favour by being "a good Christian".

Society's judgement and the father's love

The prodigal son's father had already lost his honour in front of the villagers when he handed over to the younger son his share of the inheritance. If the father previously, had had any kind of respectable status in the village community, he surely lost it after the son had disgraced him. The whole village had to carry the shame, for the shame of that father would be talked about even in the neighbouring villages.

According to the honour killing tradition the villagers, without doubt, would lynch the son, if he had the impudence to show up anywhere near the village. Therefore, the father runs towards his son to make sure he will be there before the villagers. First, a grown man does not normally take any running steps in the Middle East. Children and servants run, not self-respecting men. The father of this story, however, lifts his skirts to his belt when he sees his son far away on the edge of the village. The prodigal son's father then becomes the object of derision when he is seen running legs flashing along the village street to meet his son. Secondly, he takes on the son's shame in order to protect him from the wrath of the villagers. In this story, the father therefore, carries the shame of his good-for-nothing son many times over, in order to protect him from the wrath of the villagers.

When the son then starts his speech for his father, he manages to say only the two first points of his speech, where he confesses to his father what he has done wrong. Just when the son draws his breath to present his actual solution, the father interrupts his speech and declares this shabby stranger to be his son. God did not plan that we should return to Him through our own efforts. He wants to declare us His children. This is the Gospel!

The father does not reprimand his son or demand that he account for his actions. He orders his servants to quickly bring the best robe to cover the filthy rags, and sandals for his dirty feet. The cleansing operation and analysis of guilt are thus left for later. At this point covering of the shame and dressing into honour are essential. As a sign of the right of the inheritance the son also receives a ring on his finger. This is a peculiar detail, as the inheritance had already been given and squandered. The son therefore, receives a new inheritance, i.e. a new will and testament. This too also is deducted from the father's portion. The father loses everything because of his son. Jesus Christ made himself nothing and took the very nature of a servant (Phil 2:7). In Christ God becomes a slave, for us to become children. Therefore, if the Son sets us free, you will be free indeed (John 8:36).

The juxtaposition of a slave and a child is shown once more in the conversation between the father and the older son. The older son, in his agitation, reveals his heart's attitude. He had also missed merrymaking without his father. Now, that the younger son had returned home and celebrates with his father, the older brother complains that he has not been able to celebrate – with his friends! He did not miss his father's company. In addition, he declares that he has served his father faithfully like a slave. In the original language, the expression is: "all these years I have been slaving for you". In his heart, he has not been a child at all, but a slave pursuing merit. So, in the end the father only has one son, the returned prodigal son. God also, does not have any other, but prodigal children.

EATING TOGETHER CREATES A COMMUNITY

The three Biblical rules for eating

A sign of a happy family is a family coming together to dine and share the latest news. A meal creates unity. New believers from an Islamic background often ask, what they are allowed to eat. What are the food regulations? Food regulations are one of the most important means of defining a community. Thus, eating is not an insignificant matter. It is therefore important to familiarise ourselves with the Biblical teaching of the permissible and forbidden foods. Statutes have been given, in the beginning to Adam and Eve, then to Noah, and later to the people of Israel.

In the beginning God created man as a vegetarian. It is not therefore wrong to keep to a vegetarian diet. A diverse vegetarian diet is healthy and Biblical. This is the first food guideline. And God said: *"I give you every seed-bearing plant on the face of the whole earth and every tree that has fruit with a seed in it. They will be yours for food"* (Gen 1:29). In the beginning the man might have had a better genotype than now, and the flora also might then have been more diverse and nutritious than today.

To Noah, however, God gave a new command regarding food. The Bible does not explain why this change was needed. Perhaps it was a question of changed circumstances after the great upheaval. After the Flood, all nations descended from Noah's sons. They were given as food all animal flesh, only blood was forbidden to eat, because it has the life (or soul, as another translation option denotes). *"Everything that lives and moves will be food for you. Just as I gave you the green plants, I now give you everything. But you must not eat meat that has its lifeblood still in it"* Gen 9:3–4). All that moves is now food for them. This matter could not be expressed any more comprehensively. We must note that this is now God's declaration of permitted foods for the whole of humankind.

Then the Bible presents a third food regulation. Later restrictions are not in conflict with the rule that was given to Noah, for the later prohibitions only concern the people of Israel, and are for a completely different purpose. The people of Israel are given a particular law, according to which they do not eat everything that other nations eat. Forbidden are camel, hare, pig, prawn, meat cooked in milk, etc.

Say to the Israelites: "Of all the animals that live on land, these are the ones you may eat: You may eat any animal that has a split hoof completely divided and that chews the cud. There are some that only chew the cud or only have a split hoof, but you must not eat them. These are the commands the Lord gave Moses on Mount Sinai for the Israelites" (Lev 11:2–4; 27:34).

As sharp Bible readers, we must note that these words were not meant for the gentiles. Food was given as a sign for the Jews, and that made them different from the other nations. Jews were neither allowed to marry people from other nations. In this way the Jewish kitchen was holy in the way that, a gentile would not have been allowed to use the same dishes as them.

It would have been difficult to be married if you had had to keep a separate kitchen for a wife and a husband. The reason was that the Jews had to remain a separate nation and not intermix with other nations. They were kept separate and holy with the help of the food regulations. The Jews are God's chosen people. The main purpose of their existence is that the Messiah was to come from them. The Jews also had to sacrifice this Messiah. The Jews were the priest, and the Messiah was the sacrifice that the priest sacrificed. The actual main goal of Jewish food regulation then was the Messiah.

The rules are fulfilled in Jesus

The last twist came when Jesus Christ declared all food clean.

And He said to them: *"Are you so dull? He asked. "Don't you see that nothing that enters a man from the outside can make him 'unclean'? For it doesn't go into his heart, but to into his stomach, and then out of his body."* (In saying this, Jesus declared all foods clean.) Mark 7:18–19.

The point is not that God changed his mind. God is not fickle, but he has a particular purpose and time for the food regulations. When the Messiah had arrived, the Jews stopped having a role as a particular nation. Of course, the nation of Israel still has a role in the events of the end times, but the main task has now been fulfilled. Therefore, Jesus said that now, after the Messiah has arrived, the Jews and His followers were allowed to eat anything that other nations ate.

The disciples did not quite understand this. They, at first, thought that only a Jew could belong to Jesus. Soon they, however, noticed that other nations received the Holy Spirit. In the Acts, chapter 10, we are told how God taught this important principle to the first Christians. When Peter was meeting new Christians from other nations, God gave him a vision: a cloth descended from the heaven including animals forbidden to the Jews. The voice of God said: eat! Peter tried to object pleading that he is a Jew, and as a good Jew he has never touched anything unclean. However, God asked him to eat.

When he woke up, Peter drew conclusions from this vision that reached further than any food regulations: he immediately understood that all nations can belong to God. Through this we see that there is a link between the food regulations and the special role of the Jews. If God saves people from other nations, this means that God is building himself a kingdom where food regulations are not needed anymore. And the other way around: If the food regulations are not valid anymore, the door is open to all nations to join God's Kingdom. God is creating a new community which is open to all nations.

Paul taught that in this new community we are allowed to eat anything we can find in a butcher's shop. We do not need to follow the rule given to the Jews. Neither do the Jews need to follow the rule given to them, because the Messiah has arrived. Now we are returning to the rule declared at the times of Noah and relating to all nations. Therefore, Paul teaches:

"Everything is permissible" – but not everything is beneficial. "Everything is permissible" – but not everything is constructive. Nobody should seek his own good, but the good of others. Eat everything sold in the meat market without raising questions of conscience, for "The earth is the Lord's and everything in it" (1 Cor 10:23–26).

Food is clean – man is unclean

Jesus Christ said, that evil comes from a person's heart, and not from outside. In the food in itself, there is nothing unclean. The problem lies in us.

> *And again, Jesus called the crowd to him and said, "Listen to me, everyone, and understand this. Nothing outside a man can make him 'unclean' by going into him. Rather, it is what comes out of a man that makes him 'unclean'. After he had left the crowd and entered the house, his disciples asked him about this parable. "Are you so dull?" he asked. "Don't you see that nothing that enters a man from outside can make him 'unclean'? For it doesn't go into his heart but into his stomach, and then out of his body." (In saying this, Jesus declared all foods "clean".) He went on: "What comes out of a man is what makes him 'unclean'. For from within, out of men's hearts, come evil thoughts, sexual immorality, theft, murder, adultery, greed, malice, deceit, lewdness, envy, slander, arrogance and folly. All these evils come from inside and make a man 'unclean'."* (Mark 7:14–23)

So, the Lord Jesus taught, that wickedness comes from a person's heart. So, for example, alcohol does not bring evil into a person. Many Muslims think that a person in himself is good, but alcohol is like an evil spirit, which brings evil into a person from outside. According to the Bible it is more a question of the fact that an intoxicated person cannot control the evil of his heart but lets his wickedness loose.

Therefore, the Bible warns against getting drunk from alcohol: *Let us behave decently, as in the daytime, not in orgies and drunkenness, not in sexual immorality and debauchery, not in dissension and jealousy. Rather clothe yourselves with the Lord Jesus Christ, and do not think about how to gratify the desires of the sinful nature* (Rom 13:13–14). And also: *"Do not get drunk on wine which leads to debauchery. Instead, be filled with the Spirit.* (Eph 5:18). Drunkenness starts when a person's self-control starts to slacken. The problem therefore is not in alcohol, but in our sinful nature.

The Apostle Paul teaches, that different kinds of foods are permissible for us, however, not all of them are good for us: It is better not to eat meat or drink wine or to do anything else that will cause your brother to fall (Rom 14:21).

A person can then perfectly well refuse to eat pork. He can say that it is not healthy or he does not like the taste. He can say, that he is not used to eating pork. A Muslim, who has converted to Christianity from Islam, should not avoid pork in order to hide the fact the he is not a Muslim anymore. He can, however, avoid eating pork, in order not to offend a Muslim friend.

Wine can of course, be received during the communion. Wine belonged to celebrations in Jesus' life, and wine was drunk, for example, at the wedding in Canaan. We should never get drunk, because then we would lose control of what we are doing. If alcohol bothers a friend, it would be better not to touch alcohol, even if we for our part know our limits, and alcohol does not present us with a problem.

The life is in the blood

We will return to one more detail. God gave Noah a law according to which man cannot eat blood. We know, however, that in all meat there is some blood or elements, blood plasma etc. From this we can understand, that the fact that blood is prohibited, cannot be an issue of being chemically clean from any trace of blood, rather the issue is the symbolic meaning of blood. God forbids the eating of blood, because it has life. Jesus is the goal and final point even of this rule. At the last meal Jesus took the wine cup and said: "This is my blood. Drink from this all of you."

Then he took the cup, gave thanks and offered it to them, saying, "Drink from it, all of you. This is my blood of the covenant, which is poured out for many for the forgiveness of sins" (Matt 26:27–28).

Thus, Jesus encourages us to drink blood. Noah forbid and Jesus commanded. In addition, Jesus Christ taught, that if we desire eternal life, we should drink His blood. Jesus said to them, *"I tell you, I will not drink of this fruit of the vine from now on until that day when I drink it anew with you in my Father's kingdom.* (Matt 26:29). There is indeed life in the blood. Jesus will live eternally. He has the right to enter heaven to be with God. If we want to have the life of Jesus, we must drink His blood. By accepting Jesus into our hearts, He will live in us.

> *So, Jesus said to them: "I tell you the truth, unless you can eat the flesh of the Son of Man and drink his blood, you have no life in you. Whoever eats my flesh and drinks my blood has eternal life, and I will raise him up at the last day. For my flesh is real food and my blood is real drink. Whoever eats my flesh and drinks my blood remains in me, and I in him. Just as the living Father sent me and I live because of the Father, so the one who feeds on me will live because of me."* (John 6:53–57)

In this way Jesus creates a new community into which we are joined through faith in Him. At the Lord's Supper, we come together as God's family committing ourselves to Christ and each other. Together we form an entity, which the Bible describes as the body of Christ. Christ is the head and the congregation is His body. At the Lord's Supper, we are partakers of His blood flow and life.

God has a task for the Jewish nation all the way until the end of the times, although with regard to the salvation that nation has already completed its task. From the point of view of the Gospel, even Jews do not need to follow a special diet. Islamic food regulations establish the Islamic community but point nowhere. From the point of view of the Gospel, Islamic food regulations are just misleading.

HOSPITALITY

The central common value

Generally, when we encounter a person from another religion, we look for differences. Differences are interesting. We wonder at odd things and ask why Muslims act in a particular way. Muslims often cannot explain to us, why they act as they do. It is just the way things have always been done. For themselves, it is beneficial to press for explanations and reasons. Often there are no reasons, and Islam turns out to rest on empty or rickety foundations. Concentrating on the differences, however, adds to the juxtaposition, which is not always beneficial. We might end up provoking the Muslim to defend himself and in so doing strengthen him in his own positions.

Examining the similarities is more beneficial from the point of view of the Gospel. With the help of the similarities we can build bridges, over which we can carry the Gospel to the Muslim across a divisive chasm. The bridges are not, however, meant to become "lasting structures". Lasting structures have a danger to create a new kind of religion, which would be a mongrel, monster uniting Christianity and Islam.

Therefore, the bridges have to be just like temporary scaffoldings and tools, not the actual building.

Among the most central Islamic values is hospitality. We are used to thinking that in Islamic cultures the separation of men and women is one of the central values. That does not, however, outweigh hospitality. When I, once upon a time, was distributing Gospel booklets and clothing aid amongst some Bedouin tribes, a woman walking alone was not allowed to receive a parcel from me. Gender morality demanded that the shepherd girl had to keep a distance of about 20 meters at this coincidental meeting in the desert. I had to leave the aid parcel on a stone and back off 20 meters, in order for her to be able to come and pick up my the parcel. A moment later I was a guest in a Bedouin tent and to my surprise, for a moment, I was left alone in the tent with a woman.

In a modern city culture, a Muslim woman avoids being alone with a man in his home, if he is not her husband or a close relative. She has, however, an obligation to invite into her home a lost traveller and offer food. Hospitality can then cross the rules of gender morality – such a high value is put on it. Hospitality is also a crucial tool to gain honour. A hospitable person is respected in the whole community.

When we meet people from other cultures, it is good to admire things in them that they themselves consider to be the most valuable. When we are visited by a foreigner, we have the habit of asking what he thinks of Finland and the Finnish people. This might be an example of the poor self-esteem of the Finns. If the foreign visitor knows how to compliment things of which we ourselves are proud of, we feel good and are encouraged to adhere even more to those good values. Finns are pleased if they are complimented for their perseverance, working hard and being honest. It also feels good when we are complimented due to high technology, good social security and a good educational system.

Similarly, we can compliment a Muslim for their hospitality. It is not, in fact even difficult, for Muslims can really be excellent hostesses and hosts. When travelling in Muslim countries in areas where there are hardly any other foreigners, I have received overwhelming hospitality from complete strangers. I must admit, correspondingly I have at times also received hostility and cruel treatment.

A Muslim immigrant does not receive the same level of hospitality in the West as a westerner would normally receive in a Muslim country. In the West, we have become too busy and unconcerned to show hospitality. We have externalised the love of one's neighbour to the social security system. The authorities, however, cannot in any way compensate for hospitality which has a friend's face. In the eyes of an immigrant any dealings with the authorities is faceless, and therefore in their eyes, does not count as hospitality. Hospitality is expressed by means of food and time. The more time we have to give, the more value we have shown to our guest or our host.

Love a foreigner

The point of hospitality, in the end, is all about neighbourliness towards a stranger. In the Greek New Testament, the word for hospitality is xenophilia. That word is a bit similar to the word xenophobia, which in recent years has been used a lot in the media. Xenophilia is the opposite of the hatred of foreigners and means loving a foreigner, or friendliness towards a stranger.

It is interesting to observe that the Old Testament, which on the one hand, teaches strict nationalism to the Jews, on the other hand also exhorts strict friendliness towards foreigners. *"The alien living with you must be treated as one of your native born. Love him as yourself, for you were aliens in Egypt. I am the Lord your God"* (Lev 19:34).

Strong patriotism and helping immigrants are not therefore mutually exclusive! Perhaps it is indeed so, that from the point of strong nationalistic feeling one can genuinely afford to help a destitute person from another country. In his parable about the Good Samaritan Jesus Christ teaches us who is a neighbour. In the account of chapter 10 of Luke's Gospel, the victim is an unconscious and naked person. It would have been possible to define the nationality and social status from his speech and costume. Neither was available. In the account we are presented with just a naked person without any specifications or labels. This person is presented to us as our neighbour by Jesus: any person. Everyone is valuable. Christ is like the Good Samaritan, who even at the cost of his own safety loves unselfishly. Kenneth Bailey has pointed out that in taking the bleeding, unconscious victim to the Jewish city of Jericho, the Samaritan takes a huge risk.[14]

The crowd could easily come to the conclusion that he is the attacker, and then there he would be defenceless from them in their fury. Bailey assumes that the Jews who had been listening to Jesus' parable could imagine that the Samaritan would end up sacrificing himself when helping the wounded person.

Middle Eastern hospitality includes a notion of the host being responsible with his life for his own guest. Missionaries have sometimes knowingly taken advantage of this cultural detail and managed to get themselves invited for a meal in the house of the most influential person and then, under his protection, proclaimed the Gospel to the whole village community.

The roots of hospitality

From where has such a strong view of hospitality come into Islamic cultures? Hospitality should be a particular sign of Christians, but now Muslims are bringing shame on us because of their excellence in this matter! The Bible teaches us clearly:

> *"Share with God's people who are in need. Practise hospitality"* (Rom 12:13).
>
> *"For each one should use whatever gift he has received to serve others faithfully, without complaining"* (1 Peter 4:9).

The letter to the Hebrews gives us a hint about the origin of hospitality. *"Do not forget to entertain strangers, for by doing so some people have entertained angels without knowing"* (Heb 13:2). This is Abraham's legacy. Abraham was able to show hospitality to angels. Lot was able to protect angels at the risk of his own life (Gen 19:1–8). Although the Bible teaches us that Abraham's physical legacy only belongs to the Jews, and the spiritual legacy

---

[14] Kenneth E Bailey, Through the Peasant Eyes, Grand Rapids, 1980.

only to those who believe in Jesus, there is also something Muslims have inherited from Abraham. One of these treasures is the culture of hospitality.

> *The Lord appeared to Abraham near the great trees of Mamre while he was sitting at the entrance to his tent in the heat of the day. Abraham looked up and saw three men standing nearby. When he saw them, he hurried from the entrance of his tent to meet them and bowed low to the ground.*
>
> *He said, "If I have found favour in your eyes, my lord, do not pass your servant by. Let a little water be brought, and then you may all wash your feet and rest under this tree. Let me get you something to eat, so you can be refreshed and then go on your way — now that you have come to your servant."*
>
> *"Very well," they answered, "do as you say."*
>
> *So Abraham hurried into the tent to Sarah. "Quick," he said, "Get three seahs of the finest flour and knead it and bake some bread."*
>
> *Then he ran to the herd and selected a choice, tender calf and gave it to a servant, who hurried to prepare it. He then brought some curds and milk and the calf that had been prepared and set these before them. While they ate, he stood near them under a tree.*
>
> *"Where is your wife Sarah?" they asked him.*
>
> *"There, in the tent," he said.*
>
> *Then one of them said, "I will surely return to you about this time next year, and Sarah your wife will have a son."*
>
> *Now Sarah was listening at the entrance to the tent, which was behind him. Abraham and Sarah were already very old and Sarah was past the age of childbearing. So, Sarah laughed to herself as she thought, "After I am worn out and my lord is old, will I now have this pleasure?"*
>
> *Then the LORD said to Abraham, "Why did Sarah laugh and say, 'Will I really have a child, now that I am old?' Is anything too hard for the Lord? I will return to you at the appointed time next year, and Sarah will have a son."*
>
> *Sarah was afraid, so she lied and said, "I did not laugh."*
>
> *But he said, "Yes, you did laugh."*
>
> *When the men got up to leave, they looked down toward Sodom, and Abraham walked along with them to see them on their way. Then the LORD said, "Shall I hide from Abraham what I am about to do? Abraham*

will surely become a great and powerful nation and all nations on earth will be blessed through him. For I have chosen him, so that he will direct his children and his household after him to keep the way of the Lord by doing what is right and just, so that the Lord will bring about for Abraham what he has promised him."

Then the Lord said, "The outcry against Sodom and Gomorrah is so great and their sin so grievous that I will go down and see if what they have done is as bad as the outcry that has reached me. If not, I will know."

The men turned away and went toward Sodom, but Abraham remained standing before the Lord. Then Abraham approached him and said: "Will you sweep away the righteous with the wicked? What if there are fifty righteous people in the city? Will you really sweep it away and not spare the place for the sake of the fifty righteous people in it? Far be it from you to do such a thing—to kill the righteous with the wicked, treating the righteous and the wicked alike. Far be it from you! Will not the Judge of all the earth do right?"

The Lord said, "If I find fifty righteous people in the city of Sodom, I will spare the whole place for their sake."

Then Abraham spoke up again: "Now that I have been so bold as to speak to the Lord, though I am nothing but dust and ashes, what if the number of the righteous is five less than fifty? Will you destroy the whole city for lack of five people?"

"If I find forty-five there," he said, "I will not destroy it."

Once again, he spoke to him, "What if only forty are found there?"

He said, "For the sake of forty, I will not do it."

Then he said, "May the Lord not be angry, but let me speak. What if only thirty can be found there?"

He answered, "I will not do it if I find thirty there."

Abraham said, "Now that I have been so bold as to speak to the Lord, what if only twenty can be found there?"

He said, "For the sake of twenty, I will not destroy it." Then he said, "May the Lord not be angry, but let me speak just once more. What if only ten can be found there?"

He answered, "For the sake of ten, I will not destroy it."

When the Lord had finished speaking with Abraham, he left, and Abraham returned home. (Gen 18:1–33)

For Abraham, offering several plentiful dishes out of hospitality was important. When any visitors happened to arrive, everything had to be the best that could be found in his household. Part of the hospitality is to play the game of modesty. Abraham belittles his own hospitality and talks about a mere cup of water, but then gives the order to quickly prepare a banquet. Even in the West we say about gifts: "You shouldn't have." or "This is far too much." And if we are being offered coffee, we will first say: "Please, you don't need to prepare anything." After a moment we give in: "Perhaps I shall just have a half a cup then." Finally, after persuasion we'll say: "Well, why not – I'll have another cup, too." The hostess herself often underrates her coffee to be too weak, or the buns to be too dry. There is something childishly funny about this game, although something poignantly beautiful, as well.

Hospitality is a spiritual event

The hospitality offered by Abraham has also a deep spiritual dimension. First, we are told that Abraham saw three men approaching his tent (Gen 18:2). One of these three speaks with Abraham (Gen 18:10). Then it is revealed that this one is God Himself (Gen 18:13). In our Bible translation this Lord who was mentioned, is in the original language Yahweh (YHWH). The other two who travel to see Lot, are in fact angels (Gen 19:1).

In Abraham's hospitality the point is not, therefore, just friendliness towards a foreigner. Hospitality for him means encountering God. Jesus Christ says this same thing slightly differently in his picture of the last judgement: "Whatever you did for one of the least of these brothers of mine, you did for me" (see Matt 25:31–46). The point is not, therefore that instead of believing in Jesus we would be offered an alternative way to God. No, but hospitality, precisely could be the way through which we can meet Jesus and believe in Him.

Showing hospitality gives Abraham a head start to boldly speak to Yahweh. Abraham starts an Oriental type of bargaining concerning a deal about the cities of Sodom and Gomorrah. An unrelenting bargaining session starts. Abraham haggles with God for mercy for these cities. Abraham presents a certain number of righteous people for the price of grace. We can imagine how this question delighted God. Finally, after he has managed to drop the price of redemption to ten righteous people, Abraham dares not bargain anymore. With his bargaining Abraham is approaching the correct direction of the heart of the Gospel, but is not brave enough to guess, what God's final price would be.

The Gospel reveals us that for one righteous person God is willing to save the sinners of the whole world. In reality, there is only one who is righteous – Jesus Christ – but that is sufficient.

Hospitality is a picture of the Gospel

Jesus Christ encourages us to use hospitality as a means of mission work:

> *After this the Lord appointed seventy-two others and sent them two by two ahead of him to every town and place where he was about to go. He told them, "The harvest is plentiful, but the workers are few. Ask the Lord of the harvest, therefore, to send out workers into his harvest field. Go! I am sending you out like lambs among wolves. Do not take a purse or bag or sandals; and do not greet anyone on the road. "When you enter a house, first say, 'Peace to this house.' If someone who promotes peace is there, your peace will rest on them; if not, it will return to you. Stay there, eating and drinking whatever they give you, for the worker deserves his wages. Do not move around from house to house. "When you enter a town and are welcomed, eat what is offered to you. Heal the sick who are there and tell them, 'The kingdom of God has come near to you.'* (Luke 10:1–9)

The evangelists sent by Jesus are guests in a new town. The Lord Jesus advises the preachers to rely on hospitality. When the preaching is rewarded, there will be appreciation and sharing on both sides. When a person receiving the Gospel is allowed to show hospitality, he himself will be honoured. When I was young I took part in a short-term mission in Israel and noticed that despite being westernised, the Jews had a strong tradition of hospitality. On the one hand the Jews reacted in a hostile way to us Christians who were distributing gospel literature, yet on the other, I was given food, money and offers of accommodation so much that I could have lived from the hospitality. In the same vein in London where I was a missionary at the time, when I had received a team of young people to help with the door to door visiting, people from the local mosque brought us butter, meat and other groceries by the pound. Jesus' advice is to receive thankfully everything good that those proclaiming the gospel are offered. Paul was careful not to be a burden to those to whom he preached the Gospel, but on the other hand received equipment and supplies for his journeys, and hospitality at the destination. He saw that by accepting love gifts he helped the donors to receive riches from God (Phil 4:12–19).

Reciprocity is honourable

Our Lord Jesus sent his disciples on their journey, specifically without any extra shoes or a purse. If they had been well equipped, they would not have needed hospitality. In the beginning the missionaries were poor. Paul, the missionary, collected a donation from the mission field for the poor mother church in Jerusalem (Rom 15:26). In our times, we take it for granted that a country that sends missionaries is rich and the mission field is poor. In the beginning, however, it was the other way around. The strategy of Jesus was poor missionaries and a hospitable mission field. In this way in mission work we ensure reciprocity and dignity. Through reciprocity the receiver's dignity is kept. Hospitality was part of the spreading of the Gospel during the early church. *"When she and the members of her household were baptised, she invited us to her home: If you consider me a believer in the Lord", she said, "Come and stay at my house." And she persuaded us* (Acts 16:15). Jesus also was a frequent visitor and dined here and there in people's homes (Matt 9:10; Matt 26:18; Mark 2:15–16; Luke 5:29; Luke 7:36; Luke 11:37; Luke 14:1). Dining together is even today a very fundamental part of mission work. At the dinner table, we can open the discussion, perhaps on how Abraham came to encounter God through hospitality. In most cases, Jesus Christ, presents the Gospel through parables. Many of these parables use the dynamics of hospitality. The Gospel is told from two different points of view. In the parables Jesus is both a visitor and the host. Let us look at Jesus as a visitor first.

Receiving Jesus

The Lord Jesus came into this world as a human being. Although He came from outside, this world is not strange or unfamiliar to him. He is actually its owner. But he was treated like a stranger and foreigner. *"He came to that which was his own, but ..."* (John 1:11). Even as a small child Jesus ended up as a refugee in another country, because His life was threatened. In one story Jesus compares the situation to a vineyard, where the owner sends his servants and finally his son to collect his outstanding accounts, and whom the tenant farmers of the vineyard then decide to kill (Luke 20:9–15). In all these parables, the same pattern will be repeated: Jesus comes like a stranger who expects to be treated as a pleasant and honoured guest, but He is received with rejection and contempt.

Perhaps the most touching of these Bible passages is the verse in Revelation: "Here I am! I stand at the door and knock. If anyone hears my voice and opens the door, I will come in and eat with him, and he with me" (Rev 3:20).

In its original context, this verse is spoken to the church. A disconcertingly sad situation is then the fact that Jesus hopes to enter the church. It is probably not wrong to apply this to a nation, family or an individual person. When we receive Jesus with hospitality, it will result in fellowship over a meal.

Jesus Christ calls us

If we have responded to the call of our Lord Jesus and given Him space in our lives, He has become our guest. Perhaps we have, figuratively speaking, shown Him his own place, keeping him in the guest room, but not allowing him into the private rooms of our life. We have offered Him that cup of tea and a couple of biscuits found in the cupboard, and hope He will now be satisfied.

Part of the hospitality, however, is reciprocity. If we are invited to a Muslim's home, and enjoy a tasty dinner with him, there is an expectation to invite him to our home. In this way, the friendship becomes stronger through visits to each other's homes. In this way, we can expect that also Jesus, after receiving that cup of tea in our lives, invites us to him. This is exactly what he does. He invites us to a wedding celebration in his Father's house. There will be a grand celebration with people from east and south (Luke 13:29).

We are now at the point in our lives where Jesus Christ has become a guest in our midst and has promised to invite us to Him. He is preparing a place for us in His Father's home. *"Do not let your hearts be troubled. Trust in God, trust also in me. In my Father's house are many rooms; if it were not so, I would have told you. I am going there to prepare a place for you. And if I go and prepare a place for you, I will come back and take you to be with me that you may also be where I am"* (John 14:1–3).

He wants us to be where He is now: with his Father.

I have, on numerous occasions, in the Middle East sat down in the back row in a large room and by the door in a private home. Somebody has always come and taken me by the hand and shown me to an honoured guest seat. In these homes people usually sit on mattresses on the floor in the living room. The mattresses are spread along the room's walls. The lowest place is by the door and the highest place along the wall opposite the door right next to the host. You can imagine yourself having been lifted higher to sitting at that place of honour and telling about the advice of Jesus to sit on a lower place from which you can be elevated. Then you will continue by telling that Jesus has invited us to a great celebration, where he has already determined our sitting place.

In the Islamic culture the greatest honour is not to be invited, but to receive a guest. A guest respects the host by becoming his visitor. It certainly is an unfathomable honour to be invited to a heavenly celebration. However, even more unfathomable is that some have the nerve to refuse the invitation. *"The kingdom of heaven is like a king who prepared a wedding banquet for his son. He sent his servants to those who had been invited to the banquet to tell them to come, but they refused to come"* (Matt 22:2–3).

There are people in Finland who have scorned the invitation to the Independence Day banquet at the Presidential Palace. In the Muslim culture one could not act in such an offensive way. It is difficult to imagine how anyone could miss a royal wedding. Now, the one who invites is God himself! This view presented by Jesus practically compels a Muslim to believe in Jesus.

At receiving an important invitation, we will cancel everything else and make this invitation a priority. If our Muslim friend understands the invitation of Jesus, it is essential that he puts all Islamic teachings aside. Jesus has honoured us by coming to us. We honour him by responding to his invitation. By rebuffing the invitation of Jesus, the Son of God, we offend God. By declining we disgrace God and steal his honour.

A reluctant host

Once Jesus was an invited guest at a house of a Pharisee.

> *When one of the Pharisees invited Jesus to have dinner with him, he went to the Pharisee's house and reclined at the table. A woman in that town who lived a sinful life learned that Jesus was eating at the Pharisee's house, so she came there with an alabaster jar of perfume. As she stood behind him at his feet weeping, she began to wet his feet with her tears. Then she wiped them with her hair, kissed them and poured perfume on them.*
>
> *When the Pharisee who had invited him saw this, he said to himself, "If this man were a prophet, he would know who is touching him and what kind of woman she is—that she is a sinner."*
>
> *Jesus answered him, "Simon, I have something to tell you."*
>
> *"Tell me, teacher," he said.*
>
> *"Two people owed money to a certain moneylender. One owed him five hundred denarii, and the other fifty. Neither of them had the money to pay him back, so he forgave the debts of both. Now which of them will love him more?"*
>
> *Simon replied, "I suppose the one who had the bigger debt forgiven."*
>
> *"You have judged correctly," Jesus said.*
>
> *Then he turned toward the woman and said to Simon, "Do you see this woman? I came into your house. You did not give me any water for my feet, but she wet my feet with her tears and wiped them with her hair. You did not give me a kiss, but this woman, from the time I entered, has not stopped kissing my feet. You did not put oil on my head, but she has poured perfume on my feet. Therefore, I tell you, her many sins have been forgiven – as her great love has shown. But whoever has been forgiven little loves little."*

Then Jesus said to her, "Your sins are forgiven."

The other guests began to say among themselves, "Who is this who even forgives sins?"

Jesus said to the woman, "Your faith has saved you; go in peace."
(Luke 7:36–50)

Jesus points out that as a host the Pharisee had acted in an offensive way towards his guest. The Pharisee was probably in a difficult situation. As a religious dignitary, his duty was to invite an itinerant rabbi to his house. It was part of his honourable status in the society. If he had neglected hospitality, he would have lost part of his own honour. On the other hand, by showing unreserved hospitality to Jesus he, at the same time, ended up giving an endorsement to the proclamation of Jesus. Therefore, he ended up showing hospitality in a way that at the same time demonstrated that Jesus was not really welcome. He played the social game very skilfully and probably congratulated himself over his clever solution. Jesus pronounces aloud the three things by which the host had shamed him:

1. The guest was not given any water to wash his feet.
2. He was not welcomed by a kiss on the cheek.
3. His head was not anointed with oil.

All these would have been expressions of normal hospitality.

Although Jesus was fed, He declares the Pharisee's hospitality in fact, to be non-existent. Suddenly Jesus connects hospitality directly to the forgiveness of sins. The woman who had appeared there had led a sinful life and shows her appreciation to Jesus by carrying out all three duties of hospitality. She washes the feet of Jesus with tears, greets Him by kissing His feet and anointing His feet with perfume. Jesus says that the woman's acts of love show gratitude for being forgiven for so many sins.

Jesus gets the Pharisee to acknowledge the principle according to which one who has been forgiven much, will love much, and those who have been given little, will love little. As the Pharisee's deeds of love amounted to zero, it tells us, that this Pharisee had not been forgiven at all. The shrewd social game ended up with him having said too much. He was trapped by his own cleverness.

We have no other option but to receive Jesus Christ

Muslims claim to believe in Jesus and praise Him as one of the most important prophets after Muhammed. They, however, deny that in Jesus, God himself came to us. They deny that Jesus suffered on the cross for our sins.

They dispute the fact that Jesus calls us to God in heaven. They politely pretend to believe in Jesus, like the Pharisee seemingly offering a place at the table. In fact, they deny and shame Jesus, and are left without the forgiveness of sins. However, as Jesus let the Pharisee himself realise, how inappropriately he had acted, we also should let the Muslims understand, through their stories of hospitality that they reject God himself.

We are grateful to Muslims for the fact that they themselves help us find points in the Bible to which we ourselves have been blind. Our own understanding of the Scriptures deepens, when we look at matters from the point of view of an enemy of the Gospel. In the same way as Paul calls his own people, the Jews, enemies of the Gospel (Rom 11:28), we can also regard Muslims according to the teachings of their religion, as enemies of the Gospel. However, right here with them we are being nourished: *"You prepare a table before me in the presence of my enemies"* (Ps 23:5). *"You anoint my head with oil; my cup overflows."* Our Lord feeds us, when we share His word.

The guest becomes the host

Jesus is present where there are people gathered in His name. Forty days after His resurrection, Jesus shows, what this means. When the disciples are together after the resurrection talking about Jesus, He appears in their midst in a visible and tangible way. Jesus demonstrates that He keeps his promise to be present. The same happened also on the road to Emmaus, when two disciples disappointedly discuss the day's events. Jesus appears as a stranger next to them.

Then as the evening darkens, they arrive at a house, where Jesus is invited in. Jesus does stay in the role of a guest but acts as the host. When He breaks the bread, then the disciples recognise Him. Jesus is present even now, when we meet in His name. In a special way, He is present in the Holy Communion. At that point He is not a stranger or a visitor. Our hearts warm and positively catch fire, when He makes Himself known to us. A person's whole being is right, when we can honour our Lord Jesus Christ as the host.

CLOSING WORDS

We are used to adding a doxology to the end of the Lord's Prayer: "... for yours is the kingdom, power and glory. Amen." This final sentence, according to the oldest manuscripts, might not be the way Jesus taught the Lord's Prayer. According to the ancient liturgies of Middle East Orthodox churches it is the congregation's response to the Lord's Prayer, which was read out by the priest.

We can see three world cultures in these three words of the Doxology: the kingdom, the power and the honour. The church that is made up of people from the cultures of guilt, fear and shame bring their worship to the Heavenly Father.

God's kingdom is a governing order with justice. God's kingdom is the heavenly answer to the sinfulness of the world. God's power is omnipotence, which dispels fear. His power is heaven's answer to Satan's destructive power in this world. God's honour and radiance are His answers to everything that is dark and shameful in our lives.

A person's highest aim is to bring glory to God. Following Jesus means carrying the cross. Jesus brought honour to the Father by being an obedient Son. He carried the cross and by doing so brought honour to the Father. By looking to be honoured by the world, we shame God. The shame of carrying the cross before the world honours God (John 5:44). However odd it might feel, in the end we will bring the highest honour to God by agreeing to his invitation to come to Him into the eternal joy of heaven.

As a child, I learned the Lord's Prayer by heart. It became a habit, which became, in an inexplicable way important. With the evening prayer, there was another routine. I called my father or mother: "Come and cover me!" Tightly wrapped up in the cover I felt safe to fall asleep.

Moses was blessed to have the experience of being covered. Moses was brave enough to ask God to see His brightness and glory (Exod 33:18–23). God warned Moses: "...for no-one who sees me will live." But God liked the fact that Moses desired to see Him. So, He hid him in a cleft in the rock, put His hand on him and passed by. Moses was able to hide in Christ the rock and be covered by God's right hand, Jesus Christ. Moses lacked nothing. Moses was able to experience God's glory well covered.

We can ask in our evening prayer: "Father, into your hands I commit my spirit." We can safely pray the Old Testament Jewish prayer that Jesus said on the cross (Luke 23:46): Father, into your hands I commit my spirit.

In you, o Lord, I have taken refuge;
let me never be put to shame;
deliver me in your righteousness.
Turn your ear to me,
come quickly to my rescue;
be my rock of refuge, a strong fortress to save me.
Since you are my rock and fortress,
for the sake of your name,
lead and guide me.
Free me from the trap, that is set for me,
for you are my refuge.
Into your hands I commit my spirit;
redeem me, O Lord, the God of truth. (Ps 31:2–6)

Bert de Ruiter (ed.)

Engaging with Muslims in Europe

In Europe one finds Christian communities and Muslim communities living in close proximity to each other. Muslims and Christians pass each other in the streets, stand next to each other waiting for the bus or metro, live next to one another in streets, share apartment buildings with each other, study in the same universities, have their lunches in the same business canteens, shop in the same shopping centres. Nevertheless, they are essentially strangers to each other. Only a small minority of Churches and Christians in Europe are engaged with Muslims through meaningful and loving relationships which provide opportunities to witness to them about the truth of God.

The European Ministry to Muslims Network of the European Leadership Forum seeks to equip the Church in Europe to relate to Muslims with a compassionate heart, an informed mind, an involved hand and a witnessing tongue. In this book members of the network and others write about their engagement with Muslims in Europe.

Pb. • pp. 112 • £ 7.00 • $ 12.00 • € 8.00
ISBN 978-3-95776-025-8

VTR Publications • Gogolstr. 33 • 90475 Nuremberg • Germany
info@vtr-online.com • http://www.vtr-online.com

Bert de Ruiter

Sharing Lives

Overcoming Our Fear of Islam

Many European Christians fear that Europe will gradually turn into Eurabia, or Islamic domination of Europe, and they ignore the efforts of Muslims to adapt to the European context, a situation pointing to a future scenario of Euro-Islam, or Islam being Europeanized. The author argues that instead of an attitude of fear, which leads to exclusion, Christians should develop an attitude of grace, which leads to embrace.

The author developed a short course to help Christians overcome their fear of Islam and Muslims and to encourage Christians to share their lives with Muslims and to share the truth of the Gospel.

Pb. • pp. XIII + 209 • £ 13.95 • $ 22.95 • € 14.90

ISBN 978-3-941750-22-7

Sharing Lives

Course book

A course to help Christians share their lives with Muslims

Available in
English (978-3-95776-202-3), **Africaans** (978-3-95776-205-4), **Dutch** (978-3-95776-203-0), **Finnish** (978-3-95776-209-2), **French** (978-3-95776-208-5), **German** (978-3-95776-201-6), **Hungarian** (978-3-95776-204-7), **Italian** (978-3-95776-206-1), **Portuguese** (978-3-95776-210-8), **Romanian** (978-3-95776-211-5), **Russian** (978-3-95776-212-2) and **Spanish** (978-3-95776-207-8).

Pb. • ca. 80 pp. • £ 7.50 • $ 12.00 • € 9.50

www.ingramcontent.com/pod-product-compliance
Ingram Content Group UK Ltd.
Pitfield, Milton Keynes, MK11 3LW, UK
UKHW021654190726
13853UKWH00001B/247

9 783957 762009